TREES
of the world

TREES
of the world
Scott Leathart

A & W Publishers, Inc.,
New York

Contents

Introduction

Without trees the world would be a bleak place for man and beast alike. Indeed, life as we know it would be impossible. Fortunately, they have been growing on our planet in various shapes and forms for nigh on 400 million years and over eons of time life has evolved beneath their ever-changing canopy. They have tempered the impact of the sun, the wind, and the rain, and the Earth's supply of life-giving oxygen has been maintained by their constant exhalations.

The extent, the magnitude, and the time scale of the vast forests of gigantic, fern-like trees which once covered so much of the Earth's surface can in some measure be comprehended by the estimate that 4 centimetres of coal lying compressed beneath the ground represent 1000 years of accumulated forest growth and decay; and some of the coal seams are hundreds of metres thick, with the world's reserves of coal at workable depths estimated at 10 million million tonnes.

In modern times, trees remain the guardians of our soil and water, the homes and refuges of wild life, the providers of many things without which modern life could not proceed, our only renewable source of carbon and, of immediate and daily importance, things of ever-changing beauty. It is their grace and form, the silent almost timeless vigil which their long lives give them over man's succeeding generations, their links with the past, their hopes for the future which give trees an especial attraction to many of us. This book is for them and for those who will join their ranks. But none of us, whether we care for trees or not, could live our present lives without them.

The tree as an individual

A tree is generally considered to be a woody, perennial plant with a single stem or trunk which, some distance from the ground, produces limbs or branches, and grows to a height of not less than 4 to 6 metres (13 to 20 feet). Some trees produce two or more trunks and others, such as palms, have no branches. Furthermore, an exposed site or a rocky soil may stunt a tree which would in better circumstances grow much bigger. Thus, there can be no hard and fast rule, but in this book we have included only those trees which attain a minimum height of 7·5 metres (25 feet) in average conditions and for only a small proportion of those can we find space here.

For conciseness and clarity it is hard to fault the military description of the only three types of trees which soldiers recognize—the palm tree, the fir tree, and the bushy topped tree. These coincide with three more elegant terms often used to describe trees in general—columnar, excurrent, and deliquescent. Few trees fail to fit into one of these groups.

A tree, like any other plant, starts life as a seed which, influenced by moisture and warmth, germinates, pushing forth a root downwards and a stem upwards. The root anchors the plant and extracts water and dissolved mineral salts from the soil, and the stem bears branches and leaves in the air and sunlight where they manufacture carbohydrates essential to the growth and well-being of the tree.

In many perennial plants the stem with its leaves performs an annual function, then perishes, dries up, and falls to the ground leaving only roots and a residual stem to ride out the winter's inhospitable months. But a tree shoot does not die; it becomes hard and woody, forming along its length well-protected buds within which the next year's shoots and leaves are wrapped against frost, wet, and drying winds.

Top
Palm tree (columnar).
Centre
Fir tree (excurrent).
Bottom
Bushy topped tree (deliquescent).

Thus does a tree grow year by year, pushing upwards, always with an advantage each spring over its herbaceous rivals which, although they grow quicker, are forever back to the beginning each autumn. Even the woody shrubs are eventually overtaken as the tree's annually lengthening and thickening stem reaches upwards until, in course of time – time which matters little to a plant so well adapted to survival – the tree spreads out above all its competitors and, with others of its kind, rules supreme.

This life at the top cannot be supported without special adaptations. The taller a tree grows the more support it needs. Thus, it produces extensive anchoring roots to hold it upright and myriads of feeding rootlets to supply the leaves with water and salts. To support this huge food factory and present the surface of each leaf to its source of power, sunlight, an intricacy of spreading branches and twigs must constantly increase. To hold this great complex of fluttering, moisture-laden leaves 30 metres (100 feet) or more above the ground and to pipe water up and down, a sturdy, resilient trunk must be formed and thickened year by year. And, as the tree reaches maturity, so does the ultimate task of all living things – reproduction – press upon it, adding yet more to the weight it has to carry. All over its spreading canopy flowers, fruits, and ultimately seeds are produced. Seeds are often borne in immense and seemingly wasteful numbers.

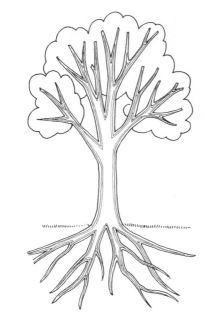

A diagrammatic tree showing the inner xylem and outer phloem through which nutrients and sugars flow up and down, respectively.

The roots

The first root which the seedling tree pushes into the soil becomes its anchor during the early years of growth and from it lateral roots radiate, those near the surface forming a horizontal platform which supports the tree and distributes the pulling strain caused by wind. From these lateral roots and others deeper down an ever-finer spreading network of rootlets weaves and twists among all the mineral and organic matter which makes up the soil, ending in root hairs which insinuate themselves between the smallest soil particles extracting water and nutrients.

The tenacity with which the anchoring or tap root holds to the surrounding soil is demonstrated by how difficult it is to pull up even a small oak seedling, and the amount of space which a tree's roots take up in the soil, especially the fibrous rootlets and the root hairs, can be appreciated by the fact that an oak tree's roots in a deep soil very often penetrate as far down as the tree is tall; while in a rocky, shallow soil they spread sideways over an area much in excess of that covered by the spread of the branches.

In addition to the two main functions – support for the tree and the extraction of water from the soil – roots also act as storage space for foodstuffs manufactured as sugars in the leaves and converted to starches under ground.

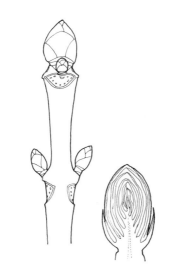

Left
Winter resting buds of the Horse Chestnut. Note the horseshoe-shaped leaf scars.
Right
Cross-section of winter bud showing folded embryo leaves.

The trunk

The trunk of a tree, in addition to supporting the crown, connects the roots to the leaves. Within it, just beneath the bark, are two sets of pipes or vessels: the **xylem**, up which water and nutrients flow from the roots to the leaves, and the other, called the **phloem**, down which manufactured sugars flow from the leaves to the roots. These pipes are formed on either side of a layer of cells immediately beneath the bark, called the **cambium**.

In the spring when the cambium starts its work, the woody vessels grow large and thinned walled, to carry the sap necessary for the intense activity of bud bursting and leaf growth, but during the summer they become smaller with thicker walls. Thus, there is a visible difference between the **spring wood** and the **summer wood**. This difference in colour and texture creates the annual rings. Such rings are only obvious in trees which have a growing season caused by changes in temperature or drought, and are not easily seen in trees which grow steadily throughout the year such as those in tropical rainforests.

The woody vessels and cells do not perform their sap-conducting function throughout the life span of the tree. After some years, perhaps ten or fifteen, they die and become embalmed in tannins or resins, darkening in colour. This change forms the **heartwood** of the tree which serves only as support, and is the timber of commerce. Beyond the outer layer of vessels, which performs no other function than that of conducting sap downwards, is another cambium producing the tree's

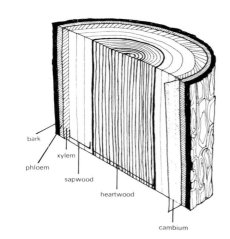

bark
phloem
xylem
sapwood
heartwood
cambium

Cross-section of a tree trunk.

protective coat or **bark** which may be thin and papery as in birches or rough and fibrous, several centimetres thick and fireproof, as in redwoods.

The leaves

The leaves of a tree which may be all sorts of shapes and sizes – long and thin in conifers, usually broad and sometimes a compound of leaflets in hardwoods – are wonderfully intricate appendages, covered with thousands of tiny, adjustable openings, called **stomata**, through which carbon dioxide is taken in from the air. As we have seen, water passes into the roots of the tree and thence through the xylem to the cells in the leaves. The carbon dioxide which has also come into the cells via the stomata, dissolves in the water and the carbon, together with the hydrogen and oxygen in the water, and aided by a green substance called **chlorophyll**, react together to form simple carbohydrates which, when subsequently conveyed to the trunk and roots, are converted into more complex substances such as starches, fats and proteins – all very necessary for the growth and well-being of the tree. This remarkable process called **photosynthesis**, which takes place in the leaves, shows how vital are those organs to the tree. Without them no growth could take place. Indeed, the leaves of all green plants are one of the fundamentals of life on Earth, because all life directly or indirectly depends upon them for food. There is another important function which leaves perform – that of purifying the atmosphere. They absorb air containing carbon dioxide, a gas harmful to animal life, and emit only oxygen, a gas upon which all life depends.

The shape of the leaves is probably not important from the functional point of view. Where they are long and narrow they will be great in number, and where they are large and broad they will be fewer, but the surface area presented to the sunlight will be about the same for any given set of climatic conditions. The structure of the leaf surface is important. Where sunlight is balanced by a sufficiency of water, the leaves tend to have matt surfaces and are wafer thin; but where sunlight is intense and the air dry, leaves have tough, shiny surfaces and are much thicker, so that they reflect the light, and moisture is retained in the well-protected cells.

As an additional defence against cold, and sometimes against heat and wind, the leaves of many trees cease functioning at certain times, dry up, and drop off only to be replaced when conditions again become favourable. Such trees are called **deciduous**. **Evergreens**, too, change their leaves at equally regular but wider-spaced intervals, but as they are always replaced before they fall the trees remain fully fledged throughout the year always ready to take advantage of the sudden onset of a possibly short growing season.

Flowers and fruits

All trees have flowers in one form or another: they are the sexual organs. They may be male or female, or both together, and they may be carried singly or on special structures bearing many flowers. In some trees, such as Monkey Puzzles, willows, and hollies, individuals are male or female and very rarely both at once. But, wherever the flowers are placed on the tree and in whatever form they are carried, the male flowers or male parts of the flowers, the **stamens** all produce **pollen**, and the females all have within them **ovules** which must be fertilized (pollinated) by the pollen before growth of the embryo can begin. This pollination is all done quite by chance; in many trees by the wind, in others by insects and, in some special cases, by birds and bats, all attracted by the flowers in their search for food, and carrying the pollen, accidentally dusted on them, from one flower to another.

Once the seeds start to grow, the capsules or ovaries in which they are contained begin to expand and eventually become hard and dry, or fleshy. In the case of conifers which have no ovaries, the scales of the cones envelop the seeds in a sealed, resinous globule. The object of these 'fruits' which grow from the female flowers, is firstly to provide a safe, dry, insulated place in which the seeds may develop and secondly, when they have developed, to ensure by one means or another that the seeds become dispersed as far away from the parent tree as is possible. Thus, they may be fitted with wings, or parachutes or simply with a downy appendage which gives them a buoyancy in the air and a chance of

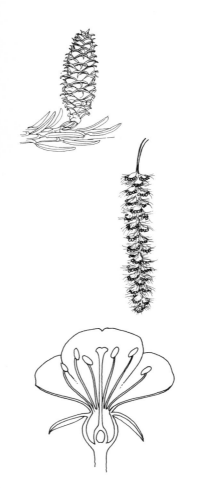

being carried far afield by the wind. Or the fruits may become attractive as food to animals which may carry them and accidently drop them (Jays and acorns), bury them in stores and forget where they are (squirrels and hazel nuts) or, in the case of those with fleshy surrounds, swallow them and void the seeds wherever they will.

By whatever means this dispersal is effected, it is a chancy business, and to make sure that enough seeds find their way to a favourable spot for germination and growth trees must and do produce prodigious quantities; the more haphazard the distribution the greater the quantity.

Tree names

Many people shy away from scientific names as being beyond their comprehension and impossible to remember. But such names have their uses in preventing confusion within the English-speaking world and in ensuring accurate recognition in other countries. In this book we have grouped trees into **families** and, within families, into **genera** which are smaller groups with similar characteristics, and finally into **species** or individuals. In some cases individual species differ in certain ways, such as leaf colour or branch form, and these we have listed as **cultivars** (cultivated varieties). Thus, a Copper Beech will be shown as belonging to the family Fagaceae and it will be named *Fagus* (genus) *sylvatica* (species) 'Purpurea' (cultivar).

Some English tree names vary not only between English-speaking countries but between parts of the countries themselves; and some names are plain misleading, not to mention the confusing tags which timber merchants attach to some woods. A Sycamore is called a Plane in Scotland and a kind of fig is called a Sycamore in the Bible; a Red Cedar is nothing of the sort but a relation of the cypress; and redwood to a timber merchant is Scots Pine and not the California giant tree most of us know by this name. So there is some point in recognizing and learning scientific names which, when their English meanings are understood, are both interesting and helpful.

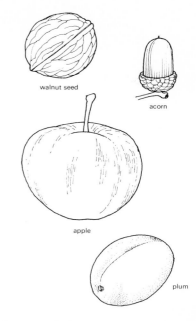

Various tree fruits.

A name plate which can be understood internationally.

Major forest zones of the world.

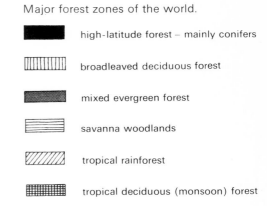

high-latitude forest – mainly conifers

broadleaved deciduous forest

mixed evergreen forest

savanna woodlands

tropical rainforest

tropical deciduous (monsoon) forest

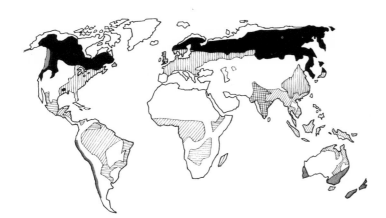

The tree as part of a community – the forest

A forest is a highly complex community of trees, shrubs, ground plants, mammals, birds, insects, and soil fauna dominated by the trees which shield all beneath them from the impact of the sun, wind, and rain. The trees may be evergreen, deciduous, or both in mixture, and the climate may be temperate or tropical; but whatever its situation and whatever its trees, a forest provides a special environment affecting the kind of plants and animals which can thrive beneath its canopy.

Forests can develop wherever the average minimum temperature in the summer months is not less than 10°C (50°F) and where the rainfall reaches a minimum of about 200 millimetres (8 inches). Above these limits there exist endless mixtures of tree species which, despite their complexity and variations, can be grouped into a number of recognizable forest types determined by climate and situation. Where one type ends and another begins may be difficult to determine with accuracy but, broadly speaking, these forest zones stretch east and west around the Earth.

High latitude forests of the northern hemisphere

These circumpolar forests, or **taiga** as they are sometimes called, form one of the most widespread forest zones in the world. They stretch almost without interruption across the north of the great continents of America and Eurasia. The trees are mainly pines, firs, spruces, and larches, with birches, aspens, willows, and alders where man, fire, or wind have created clearings. The climatic conditions are severe, the average annual temperature ranging from 4°C to 8°C (39°F to 46°F) with possible extremes from −50°C to 50°C (−58°F to 122°F). The precipitation in rain and snow varies between 200 and 300 millimetres (8 and 12 inches), fairly evenly distributed over the year.

A high latitude forest in Finland; a mixture of pines and firs, and birches and willows.

The composition of the tree mixtures and the size of the trees in these forests vary with the latitude and the soils, the pines generally favouring the lighter, sandier soils and the firs and spruces the heavier. As a rule, the further south within this zone the trees grow the taller they are. On the northern limit, bordering upon the **tundra**, trees of great age remain thin, short, and gnarled with a high proportion of dead wood, and often festooned with mosses and lichens. On the southern limits they attain considerable sizes; indeed, much of the world's softwood timber comes from these areas.

To withstand the severe conditions, these northern coniferous trees must be especially well protected against the wind and cold, and must be very modest in their demands upon the soil. Hardy conifers are conically shaped, with broad bases and tapering tops, and have short, narrow, thick, leathery leaves, with a high proportion of wood to leaves, giving them ample storage space for reserve food starches. Species such as the Scots Pine (*Pinus sylvestris*), Siberian Fir (*Abies sibirica*), Norway Spruce (*Picea abies*), as well as the American White Spruce (*Picea glauca*) and Balsam Fir (*Abies balsamea*), to mention a few, are well able to withstand the winds, frosts, and snows, and take advantage of a growing season which is never more than three months and is often as little as one.

Douglas Firs in the Cathedral Grove, Vancouver Island. These immense trees give an idea of the erstwhile magnificence of the virgin forests of the Pacific coast of North America.

Moist conifer forest of the north-west American coast

This forest zone which, unlike the others, runs north and south, is unique in the size and profusion of temperate trees which it supports. The moist winds of the Pacific coast provide an equable climate with precipitation, much of it in the form of mists and fogs, considerably greater than anywhere in the higher latitude zone. As a result, the forests of Sitka Spruce (*Picea sitchensis*), Douglas Fir (*Pseudotsuga menziesii*), pines, cypresses, and Redwoods (*Sequoia sempervirens*) are of unequalled luxuriance and are, perhaps, the most spectacular and beautiful of any in the world. These forests are prodigious in their production of timber.

In the extreme north of the zone, towards Alaska, the forest is less luxuriant and productive, while in the south the same gradual impoverishment merges into semidesert in Lower California. To the east too, up in the drier Cascade Ranges, tree growth falls off and the forests become more open. Here, as an exception to prove the rule, the biggest trees in the world, the Big Trees or Wellingtonias (*Sequoiadendron giganteum*) grow in isolated groves more than 1800 metres (6000 feet) above the sea, and the world's oldest living things, the Bristle Cone Pines (*Pinus aristata*) have clung living to the mountain tops for more than 4000 years.

Middle latitude broadleaf deciduous forest

The cool, temperate deciduous forest zone is the predominant feature of our northern countries, except on the higher ground. These forests range over the greater part of central and western Europe, north of the Alps and the Pyrenees and eastwards across Russia in a belt between the northern coniferous forests and the southern steppes, dying out towards the Urals and reappearing in the Amur region, in parts of China, and in Japan. In North America they are best developed on either side of the Appalachian Mountains, westward to the Mississippi and north to the Great Lakes. In the southern hemisphere they are much less prevalent with only small stretches, mostly of southern beeches (*Nothofagus* spp) in the extreme south-west of South America. In Africa, Australia, and New Zealand they scarcely exist.

A cool, temperate, moist climate characterizes the zone, with rain all the year round and comparatively low average temperatures varying between 8°C and 11°C (46°F and 54°F) with here and there extremes in winter and summer. The growing season is between 100 and 200 days and the rainfall varies between 700 and 1500 millimetres (28 and 60 inches), giving sufficient ground water and atmospheric moisture.

Evergreen eucalyptus forest covers extensive areas in Australia.

The main tree species are oaks (*Quercus* spp), beeches (*Fagus* spp), ashes (*Fraxinus* spp), maples (*Acer* spp), birches (*Betula* spp), limes (*Tilia* spp), and chestnuts (*Castanea* spp) merging into, and in mixture with, pines and other conifers in the more northern areas or where altitude makes conditions more severe. In some parts of Europe, beech forests with a uniform, close canopy exclude other species and are almost pure, but the oak forests are more open and other trees are liable to grow in mixture with them. In North America the forests are more luxuriant and contain an even greater number of species including walnuts (*Juglans* spp), hickories (*Carya* spp), tulip trees (*Liriodendron* spp), and magnolias (*Magnolia* spp).

Mixed evergreen forests of the southern hemisphere

South of the equator, in climatic zones roughly corresponding with middle latitudes in the north but with uniformly mild temperatures and moderate or even abundant rainfall of some 1500 to 2500 millimetres (60 to 100 inches), and with one or possibly two dry spells, there are ever-

green forests of considerable extent especially on the eastern seaboards of the land masses. In eastern Australia they are mainly of eucalypts (*Eucalyptus* spp) and in New Zealand of southern beeches (*Nothofagus* spp) podocarps, and dacrydiums. In South Africa, in what is left of the indigenous forest, yellowwoods (*Podocarpus* spp) are the biggest trees; and in South America Monkey Puzzles (*Araucaria*) and southern beeches form much of the forests in this zone.

Although these forests are for the most part on low ground, conditions which support them also occur on ground above 900 metres (3000 feet) on equatorial mountain ranges both north and south of the line.

Tropical rainforest

These forests span the Earth astride the equator and within them the temperature is so uniform that the annual variation of one or two degrees from around the 30°C (85°F) mark is less than that between night and day, so that in effect the night is the winter. The growing season is almost continuous and in some places it may rain every afternoon and night. In others there may be a short dry season, punctuated by thunderstorms, with a wet season, when it may rain for days or even

weeks on end. The light is dazzling above the canopy, for it is always overhead, but so thickly do the trees grow upon the ground, that only 1 per cent of it reaches the forest floor. Above is a sea of green, broken here and there by islands of gaudy colours where insects, frogs, birds, and mammals large and small are busy about their affairs. Beneath is a huge, gloomy vault crowded with pillars themselves festooned with massive creepers and parasitic plants.

The variety of trees is immense, although only four or five specimens of a species may occur in a hectare. The result is a canopy of very irregular outline constant only in its impenetrability as the crowns of the trees, rounded or egg shaped, jut out at varying heights interlocking one with the other.

That such a gloomy, damp environment is for terrestrial animals, especially man, profoundly unfavourable is obvious. Human settlements in or near them are rare and are usually of the most primitive type when areas of forest are felled and burned for agriculture and abandoned after one or two years. But Nature's reclamation of the rainforest is swift and inexorable, and the clearings are soon enveloped.

Tropical deciduous (monsoon) forest

These forests occur in the true monsoon areas of India, Burma, and Indochina and southwards to northern Australia, as well as in regions bordering the tropical rainforests of Africa, Indonesia, and South America. The characteristic climate is hot, averaging about 27°C (80°F), with a dry season lasting from four to six months. Both the diurnal and the annual ranges of temperatures are greater than in the tropical rainforest, and the rainfall is much less, varying between 1000 to 2000 millimetres (40 and 80 inches). Strong, dry winds are also a typical feature. As a result of these factors the trees grow further apart than in the rainforest and most of them shed their leaves in the dry season, although, as many of them also flower during this season, and at different times, these forests do not have the same lifeless appearance as the temperate deciduous forests in winter.

The open nature of the monsoon forests encourages an under-growth of woody shrubs and thickets of bamboo and, like the rainforest, the variety of species is enormous with a great many different trees in quite a small area, although Teak forests (*Tectona grandis*), perhaps the best-known tree of these forests, tend to be more uniform.

From earliest times man has lived and prospered in these forests where some of the most successful tropical agriculture has been developed. Oil-palms, Coffee, Maize, and Millet are important crops grown; and the Teak and other timber industries are a flourishing feature of this zone.

Savanna woodlands

This forest type, which is found in South America, east and central Africa, both north and south of the equator, in much of India and China, as well as in north-east Australia, results from a climate where the rainless period is more prolonged and the annual rainfall much less than in the monsoon areas. Although temperatures are high, often reaching 37 °C (90 °F), the rainfall can be as little as 400 millimetres (16 inches) and is never much more than 760 millimetres (30 inches). The trees are rarely more than 15 metres (50 feet) tall and often have flat, umbrella-like tops, especially the many thorny acacia species which abound in Africa. They grow far apart on grassy plains of immense extent where many of the world's largest animals roam in great herds. Apart from a few nomadic tribes who have found grazing for their animals in this zone, man has had little influence upon it. The great heat, the long drought, and the often fickle rainy season have made agriculture unrewarding.

Mangrove swamps

The mangrove swamp is the most widespread and important forest type in coastal mudflats throughout the tropics. In brackish, quiet lagoons and coastal swamps along tropical shores, especially where rivers meet the sea, mangroves form continuous forests seemingly sitting on the water at high tide but, as the water level recedes, standing on a tangle of crooked twisting roots supporting them above the black slime. These roots adapted for 'breathing' in the open air just above the water, enable these evergreen trees to survive where salt water and putrescent soil prevent all else from growing. As time goes on and the impenetrable tangle of mangrove roots develop, accumulated debris builds up above the brackish water and other trees are able to grow upon it until ultimately tropical rainforest may become established in places reclaimed from the sea by the mangroves.

Right
In the Mangrove swamps the trees stand on a tangle of twisted roots above the black slime.

Below
Trees planted around Thirlmere, Cumbria, England help to stabilize the soil and control the run-off.

Trees and man

Both in communities (or forests) and as individuals, trees are of crucial importance to man; yet man, since prehistoric times, initially heedlessly, later wantonly, and ultimately greedily, has destroyed them. Clearances for primitive agriculture in areas of marked seasonal drought created semideserts as ground water evaporated from the unprotected soil, forests of Cedars in Lebanon and beyond were virtually eliminated by heavy fellings for constructional purposes, and huge forests which at one time covered much of the Mediterranean region were ruthlessly felled by succeeding civilizations; and their regeneration was prevented by grazing animals.

In more modern times the rapacious assault upon the great conifer forests of north-west America, when all the best trees were removed and inferior ones (if any) were left to reproduce inferior offspring, depleted the area of forest and diminished the quality of the trees. And the same thing is happening now in some of the tropical forests.

Yet from past and present greed, and the ravages which it has caused, some good has come. We now know that when trees are removed from a mountainside, the soil which their roots once held firmly slips into the valley as landslides causing death and destruction; likewise snow scattered evenly throughout a forest will never accumulate in a deathly avalanche. We now know that when trees are felled in dry areas, the unprotected soil becomes progressively drier ending up as desert. We now know that if trees round lakes and reservoirs are felled the flow of water into them, no longer dissipated by the canopy, quickens and brings down silt, progressively reducing the depth of water; and we now realize that if we want to use the products of the forest we must so regulate our demands upon them that we do not deplete them, and if we do, we must replant trees where forest once grew.

Landslides cause devastation in mountainous areas following an earthquake, but forest cover on either side has stabilized the soil.

European alpine forests in the valley bottoms are often a mixture of coniferous and broadleaf trees.

This, then, is the reason for modern forestry – the growing of trees for timber. Where forests exist naturally, exploitation – the felling of all useful trees with no thought for the future – has been replaced by conservation – the felling of that volume of timber in a year or a number of years as will naturally be replaced by growth in the same period. Nor is this felling haphazard; the trees are chosen not only for their size but also for their situation, so that younger trees are given space to develop, seedlings receive light enough to start their growth, and seeds find clear open spaces in which to fall and germinate. By this careful husbandry, called **silviculture**, the forest becomes self-perpetuating, producing a known quantity of timber each year, yet always covering and protecting the soil.

Where forests have been destroyed, planting or seeding must be done to establish them again; and this takes time. A forest soil is an infinitely complex mixture of organic and inorganic matter built up over eons of time beneath a protecting canopy. When the trees are removed it is quickly destroyed by exposure to sun, dry winds, and heavy rain. Often the impoverishment is so great that trees which once grew there cannot be grown again, or will not grow well enough to produce timber. In such places, trees less demanding upon the soil and more amenable to exposure must be planted as a pioneer crop. We see this happening in upland areas of Britain. Here spruce and pines now reclothe the hillsides where oaks once grew and where oaks will grow anew when the reprotected soil regains fertility. In parts of Africa the thorn scrub is being replaced by pines from Mexico, and in New Zealand huge forests of pines from California are now established on recent volcanic soils of low fertility where only scrub once grew.

The seedling trees, even those for pioneer afforestation, are not just the offspring of any tree but are from parents selected for their size, growth rate, and their known ability to thrive in similar climatic conditions to those where their offspring will be planted. Even within a species, various races have evolved to suit certain areas and these are likely to fail when planted in another area where conditions are markedly different. For instance, a Scots Pine from continental Russia will show poor growth in western Scotland and an alpine-grown Larch will likely develop disease if planted in lowland England.

By working hand in hand with Nature to reverse the exploitation of centuries, foresters are starting to repay the debt which mankind has owed to trees since the dawn of history and before. Primitive people were dependent upon trees for many things other than fuel and shelter. Their fruits were important food, their leaves made thatched roofs, their bark provided cloth, and medicines came from trees as well as tannins, dyes, and spices.

Trees provide welcome shelter in exposed upland areas.

Without trees modern man would find much missing from his way of life despite the substitutes which now exist for wood and other tree products. Perhaps his greatest demand is pulpwood for paper, mainly newsprint, and packing materials, the use of which in developed countries is staggering in its volume and its waste.

Apples, cherries, peaches, pears, oranges and lemons, coconuts, and mangoes all come from trees, and many other fruits besides, as well as rubber, vegetable oils, spices and chocolate, resin, turpentine, and cork. But unquestionably timber and its products are vitally important and increasingly so. As irreplaceable fossil fuels are used up trees will stand out more and more as man's only renewable source of carbon and fuel.

Man cannot live by wood and fruits alone and trees do not minister only to his bodily needs; they have a vital part to play in his spiritual well-being. Deified and worshipped since prehistory as guardians of the dead and protectors of the living, and revered through the ages as links with the past and the present, trees have a place in human affections not enjoyed by many other living things. Nor is this affection born of longevity alone. The very size of trees inspires an awe unmatched by other creations and, with size, comes a variety of shapes and colours which make trees, whether placed there by man or Nature, an essential part of any sympathetic landscape.

Especially do we rely on trees for softening the harsh outlines of modern buildings and as complementary foils to our great architectural heritage. Planted along city streets, shading squares and open places, and breaking the monotony of suburban gardens by the very variety which individual owners choose to plant, trees have a vital role to play in our urban areas. Without them the lives of our town dwellers would be infinitely more drab. As indeed would our gardens from which so many of us gain such solace and where by careful planning we can have winter colours from green to gold, spring blossoms of every hue, summer greenery of great variety, and autumn tints of yellow, red, and gold.

Trees and wildlife

Most wild creatures – insects, reptiles, birds, and mammals – depend to a greater or lesser degree upon trees for food and shelter: directly for food where fruits, nuts, and leaves are the diet, and indirectly when insects are eaten. Shelter provided by trees may simply be a temporary hiding place, or somewhere to spend the night or escape from the heat of the day, or it may be a place to build a nest and bring up young. For a great many creatures the tree is the refuge, the home, and the larder; an important link in the self-perpetuating food chain. Greenflies, caterpillars, and many other insects drink the sap or eat the leaves of trees, many of them becoming prey to small birds, squirrels, and other arboreal animals, which also eat small mammals, such as mice and voles, that rely on nuts produced by trees for part of their food. Indeed, nuts and acorns provide much of the winter food eaten by birds and mammals which, during summer's abundance, prefer other creatures as their diet.

Top
Each timber has its own particular colour and grain. The west African Sapele is popular for flooring.

Above
Beech wood has characteristic, elongated, brown markings in its grain.

Right
Pines help to stabilize pit tips and cover these scars on the landscape.

Each forest type has its own distinctive animals, and the number and variety of them depend upon the amount and quality of the food available, the ease of finding it and whether or not it will be available in the winter. Likewise, the number of creatures will also depend upon the amount of shelter and moisture available in the forest. In tropical rainforests, and in the tall, dense conifer forests of north-west America there is ample shelter from the trees but there is little ground vegetation and easily accessible food is in short supply. Hence, wildlife, too, is scarce and highly specialized for life among the trees. The larger animals tend to have an acute sense of hearing at the expense of less well-developed senses of sight and smell; and the need to run or fly well is less important than an ability to climb well or grip branches firmly. In the temperate and monsoon forests where food is plentiful both on the trees and on the shrubs and ground plants which grow in such profusion beneath them, the amount and variety of wildlife are much greater; and, in addition to the true woodland animals which live out their lives in and under the trees, there are many other creatures which use the trees for shelter and for breeding places, sallying forth beyond the forest for food.

Food, shelter, and safety from enemies are the three things which all creatures must have if they are to survive and reproduce their kind. Trees as individuals and trees in communities large and small provide all three, or the conditions which result in all three, in a way which no other vegetation can. Thus, they are of vital importance to wildlife. True, animals which rely entirely on trees for all their needs are not very numerous; scarcely more so than those which rely on trees for none of them. Between these two groups is the vast majority of creatures which must have trees in or beneath which to shelter, bring up their young in safety, and find some of their food, be they Weaver Birds with nests hanging from the extremities of a Baobob tree, a fox with its earth beneath the roots of a clump of pines, or a deer with its fawn hidden in the fastness of an oakwood. A woodland environment, a place where winds are tempered, where rain falls gently, where the sun shines kindly and where the warmth and moisture are but gently dissipated, is essential for some or all of the wants of most creatures. Without trees wildlife would be scarce indeed.

Below
Rooks start building new nests or repairing old ones in the treetops long before the leaves appear.

Below right
The Orang-utan lives out its life in the dense canopy of the tropical rainforest.

The Conifers

Family Ginkgoaceae
GENUS *Ginkgo*

A genus (a corruption of the Chinese *yin kuo* silver fruit) of deciduous trees closely related to the conifers, but differing from them in their wide, fan-like, flattened leaves and by the method of fertilization, effected by motile sperms, giving them an affinity with the ferns.

There is only one species in the genus, the Ginkgo or Maidenhair Tree (*Ginkgo biloba*), now native only in a very restricted area of China but the sole survivor of a family which has remained unaltered by evolution since it grew in profusion when dinosaurs roamed the Earth millions of years ago.

This handsome and fascinating tree is easily recognized by its leaves each of which resembles a magnified pinna (or leaflet) of the Maidenhair Fern or, less poetically, a duck's foot–the name which the Ancient Chinese gave to the tree. When leafless in the winter, the tree looks somewhat gaunt and spiky. In old age the bark is grey and rough, like an elephant's hide; in young trees it is brown with corky fissures.

Ginkgos grow to a height of 27 to 30 metres (90 to 100 feet) and are excellent for town planting because their ancient lineage has given them an immunity to disease and a great resistance to air pollution.

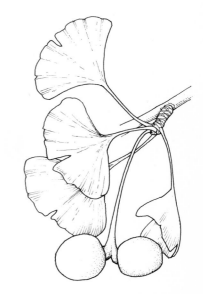

The fan-shaped leaves and the round, green fruits of the Maidenhair Tree.

Family Taxaceae
GENUS *Taxus* yews

A genus of six species of evergreen trees spread right across the northern hemisphere, distinguished by their dark green, spirally arranged leaves and their seeds borne singly in a fleshy scarlet cup.

The Common Yew (*Taxus baccata*) is native to Britain, all Europe, Algeria, and eastwards as far as northern Iran. It is a hardy tree, sombre of aspect and frequently seen of great size and age in English churchyards. Some trees are up to 1000 years old with girths as much as 9 metres (30 feet) but nearly always hollow.

The wood was used for making bows and the Yew was twice revered for its evergreen longevity and for its vital contribution to the defence of the realm. Common in the wild on chalky soils, the Yew has been much used for formal hedging and topiary work in larger gardens; and the cultivar 'Fastigiata', the Irish Yew, an upright-growing form, is often seen in gardens, as also is the gold type of this variety.

The American or Pacific Yew (*Taxus brevifolia*) is very similar in appearance to the common species, as indeed are all other yews which tend, as a family, to be divisible one from the other by their geographical distribution as much as by botanical differences. The American tree, however, has shorter, more pointed leaves with a yellowish tinge to them. The Himalayan Yew (*Taxus wallichiana*) differs so little from the common species, except that it thrives at altitudes up to 3000 metres (10 000 feet) on the mountains, that it is often considered to be merely a variety. But the Japanese Yew (*Taxus cuspidata*) has needles with a golden-brown underside and they stand almost vertically on the branches rather like the upturned wings of a bird. In the Chinese Yew (*Taxus celebica*) the needles are much more sparsely arranged on the twigs and are a paler green than in the other species.

The timber of all yews is tough, strong, and heavy. The heartwood is reddish brown and the sapwood is pale yellow, toning to a light brown with age. The colour contrasts are marked and, as the wood works well and is easily polished, it makes very attractive furniture and panelling.

Below
A Ginkgo at Penshurst Place, Kent, England. The lower leaves are assuming the yellow autumn colouring.

Right
A branch of a female Ginkgo with the maidenhair fern-like leaves and the pulpy fruits containing single nuts.

The sharp-pointed, yew-like leaves and the plum-like fruit of the California Nutmeg.

GENUS *Torreya*
(in memory of Dr John Torrey, the American botanist)

A genus of six species of yew-like, evergreen trees found in North America, China, and Japan. They differ from the yews by having much longer, more spaced-out needles with sharp points, and a green, plum-like fruit, with an outer, succulent, resinous coat and an inner woody shell.

The California Nutmeg (*Torreya californica*), so called because the fruit bears some superficial resemblance to the true Nutmeg, is a tree which reaches 27 metres (90 feet) in height in its native California where it grows sparingly along streams in the Santa Cruz Mountains and Sierra Nevada. Nor is it common in cultivation in America or Europe although, being a mountain species growing between 900 and 1800 metres (3000 and 6000 feet), it is reasonably hardy. It is an attractive tree, resembling an open-grown, pale-green yew but with longer needles and the characteristic fruit. Its relative in Florida, the unattractively named Stinking Cedar (*Torreya taxifolia*) so called because the wood and fruit has a fetid smell, is a smaller tree which grows in river swamps and is too tender to grow in Europe. As the specific name implies, the needles are more yew-like and shorter than the Nutmeg.

The Kaya (*Torreya nucifera*) from Japan differs from the American species in having bright, reddish-brown shoots and needles which are strictly parallel to one another and arched downwards. Although a tree which reaches 24 metres (80 feet) in its native Hondo Island where it is rare, it is never more than a bush in Europe. The Chinese species (*Torreya grandis*) is similarly rare both in its native Chekiang Province where it attains heights of up to 24 metres (80 feet) and in cultivation where it is seldom more than a bush.

Owing to their rarity the wood of torreyas is seldom used commercially, but it is straight grained, strong, and easy to work, and has been used for furniture and cabinet work.

Family Cephalotaxaceae

(from *kephale*, head, and *taxus*, yew, referring to the head-like male flowers)
GENUS *Cephalotaxus* cow's tail pines or plum yews

An Asiatic genus of small trees closely resembling yews but more graceful. The needles are rather like those of the torreyas but are not spined and are yellow-green in colour. The fruits, too, differ, being very like olives in shape and colour.

The Cow's Tail Pine (*Cephalotaxus harringtonia*) from China and Japan, is a small tree up to 12 metres (40 feet) tall, growing in mountain areas at between 600 and 900 metres (2000 and 3000 feet). In cultivation it is usually a small, albeit elegant bush. The needles curve upwards and inwards from the twigs like the upturned wings of a bird, with two silvery bands on the undersides. The Chinese Cow's Tail Pine (*Cephalotaxus fortuni*) is a tree of similar size confined to central China and differs from its near relative in having longer needles which are not raised upwards but are flat ranked along the twig.

The timber is yellowish and straight grained but is usually too small to be of any economic value.

Left
The upright-growing, golden Irish Yew is a popular ornamental in parks and gardens.

Above
The sombre Yew, a common sight in English churchyards.

The leathery, strap-like leaves of the Common Yellowwood.

Family Podocarpaceae

(from *podos*, foot and *karpos*, fruit, referring to the fleshy, foot-like stalk on the fruit)
GENUS *Podocarpus* yellowwoods

A genus of over 100 species of mostly tall, evergreen trees mainly confined to the warm temperate and subtropical regions of the southern hemisphere. The leaves or needles are very variable. In some species they are strap-like, hard, and leathery, in others thin and fragile, the young leaves sometimes being reddish in colour. The fruits are berry-like and green, borne on fleshy stalks.

The Common or Oteniqua Yellowwood (*Podocarpus falcatus*) is the tallest and most spectacular indigenous forest tree in South Africa, widely distributed in Cape Province, Natal, and the Transvaal. Trees of 45 metres (150 feet) tall have been recorded and in forests which have been cut over and have subsequently become protected, individual specimens can be seen towering magnificently above the other forest trees around them. Sadly, nearly all the superb trees which once abounded in the Transvaal forests were cut for the Rand mines, and the same has happened elsewhere; for the light, soft, strong, elastic, and non-resinous timber has many uses. One of the best-known specimens of this tree, still standing today in the Knysna Forest, is 42 metres (140 feet) tall with a clean bole of 21 metres (70 feet). Another South African species, the Real Yellowwood (*Podocarpus latifolius*) which has longer leaves, is similarly threatened because of its fine timber; indeed, this species has yielded more timber than any other tree in the country and was extensively used in the early pioneering days for house and wagon building.

Two Australian species, the so-called Brown Pine (*Podocarpus elatus*) and Black Pine (*Podocarpus amarus*), large, rainforest trees from the east of the country, provide a limited amount of golden-brown, finely textured timber particularly suitable for carving and turnery, but other members of the family in Australia are little more than shrubs.

Of the New Zealand podocarps the Totara (*Podocarpus totara*) is the most widespread and best known. It can reach impressive dimensions: a tree in the Totara Reserve measures 37 metres (124 feet) in · height and 6·3 metres (21 feet) in girth, a size thought to give it an age of at least 1000 years. Like the oak in Britain, the Totara in New Zealand is held in high respect because of its size and age and, again like the oak, played its part in building ships of war. From the splendid, branch-free, untapered boles 21-metre (70-foot) Moari war canoes were fashioned, and wars were even fought for the possession of individual trees. As present day timber trees they take second place only to the Kauri, the wood being red and very like mahogany in colour. Taller than the Totara but less widespread is the Kahikatea (*Podocarpus dacrydioides*), also called the White Pine and first seen by Captain Cook who measured his discovery and found it to girth nearly 6 metres (20 feet), with a bole almost 27 metres (89 feet) to the first branch. He took some trees back to England for masts, but they snapped too readily and the experiment was a failure. A tree 45 metres (150 feet) tall has been recorded, and many in reserves reach 36 metres (120 feet) and more, making this species the tallest of New Zealand's trees. Its timber is light in colour and was much used for making butter boxes.

The smaller and slimmer Matai (*Podocarpus spicatus*) or Black Pine produces a valuable timber, slow grown and fine grained, while that of the Miro (*Podocarpus ferrugineus*) or Rusty Podocarp, is similarly fine grained with dark-coloured heartwood, giving beautiful figuring to timber cut on the quarter.

About a quarter of all the podocarps come from the New World where they are mostly mountain trees ranging from Mexico to Chile and the Argentine. Although the Totara has reached heights of about 18 metres (60 feet) in Cornwall and Ireland, none of the other antipodean and South African podocarps will live in Britain. But some of the South American species, important timber trees in their own lands, seem to be hardier. The Manio (*Podocarpus nubigenus*) which reaches 24 metres (80 feet) in Chile and south Argentine, the Plum-fruited Yew (*Podocarpus andinus*) and the Willow Podocarp (*Podocarpus salignus*), both smaller trees, grow in the milder parts of Britain although, like the Totara, they rarely reach 15 metres (50 feet).

The Japanese Large-leaved Podocarp (*Podocarpus macrophyllus*) has beautiful, glossy green leaves up to 150 millimetres (6 inches) long and grows to a height of 18 metres (60 feet). It is much planted in Japan as an ornamental tree and for windbreaks, particularly near the sea. The close-grained wood is very durable and resistant to termites and is much sought after for chests and furniture. Most podocarp fruits taste of turpentine, but those of this tree are sweet and readily eaten by children. The other Japanese podocarp, the Nagi (*Podocarpus nagi*) is of similar size but with much shorter, wider leaves. The timber is inferior and the tree in general has fewer uses than the former species.

Below
The Totara, a tree held in great respect by New Zealanders because of its great size and long life.

Bottom
Kahikateas growing beside Lake Rotoroa, South Island, New Zealand. These trees were first discovered by Captain Cook.

A fine Rimu at Westland, South Island, New Zealand; it is often planted for landscaping in parks and gardens in that country.

The tiny, scale-like leaves of the Tasmanian Huon Pine.

GENUS *Dacrydium*
(from *dakrydion*, a tear, referring to resin drops)

A genus of some sixteen evergreen, cypress-like trees mainly confined to New Zealand, but also occurring in Australia, Malaysia, and Chile. The leaves are small, scale-like, and overlapping. The fruits, on the tips of the branches, resemble little acorns. The bark is brown to greyish and scaly.

The Rimu (*Dacrydium cupressinum*) or Red Pine is widely distributed throughout New Zealand where in favourable conditions it may reach heights of 24 metres (80 feet) and girths of 4·5 metres (15 feet) but considerably less at the higher altitudes of 600 metres (2000 feet) or more where it also grows. The long, weeping branches and the conical shape, especially when young, give the tree an unusual grace, and it is often used in the landscaping of parks and gardens. The timber is reddish yellow, beautifully marked, durable, and strong, and was once used for ship building and bridges. Nowadays, large trees are in short supply but the timber is still used for furniture where the fine figuring is shown to great advantage.

The Tasmanian Huon Pine (*Dacrydium franklini*) occurs on the southern and western coasts of the island, mainly between sea-level and 150 metres (500 feet) but also up to 600 metres (2000 feet). It is not quite so tall as the New Zealand species, usually only reaching about 21 metres (70 feet), but with the same fine trunk with very little taper. It also yields a finely marked timber much used on the island for boat building and joinery, but it is also in increasingly short supply.

Most of the other members of this genus are very small trees or even prostrate alpine shrubs. Another New Zealand species, the Mountain Rimu (*Dacrydium laxifolium*), is the smallest known conifer, bearing fruit when no more than 75 millimetres (3 inches) tall. The only South American species, (*Dacrydium fonkii*), barely reaches 0·9 metres (3 feet) in height.

GENUS *Phyllocladus*
(from *phyllon*, leaf, and *kladon*, branch, referring to the leaf-like branchlets)

A genus of six evergreen trees or shrubs occurring in Tasmania, New Zealand, Borneo, and the Philippines. They are chiefly remarkable for their flattened branches, or cladodes which perform the functions of leaves and carry the female flowers and thus the little, acorn-like fruits, on their margins. The bark is thick, hard, and scaly.

The Tasmanian Celery-top Pine (*Phyllocladus rhomboidalis*) attains a height of 18 to 30 metres (60 to 100 feet) near sea-level in the western parts of the island where it is most common on undulating to flat country, although it also occurs up to 750 metres (2500 feet) with moderate growth. It is a slow-growing but attractive tree despite its frequent habit of forking and producing double trunks. The timber is heavy for a softwood and durable, but is available only in very limited quantities.

The New Zealand Tanekaha (*Phyllocladus trichomanoides*) or Celery Pine, so called like the Tasmanian species, because the 'leaves' are very like those of celery, is confined to the North Island and grows to heights of 15 to 21 metres (50 to 70 feet) with girths of up to 2·7 metres (9 feet), and unusually long, branchless boles. The straight-grained, white wood was once extensively used for building purposes and the bark has an exceptionally high tannin content. Formerly, when the saplings were to be found in large quantities, as slender rods, they found a ready market in London as walking sticks. Another New Zealand species, the Taotao (*Phyllocladus glaucus*) is a handsome but small tree rarely exceeding 9 metres (30 feet) in height.

GENUS *Saxegothaea*
(in honour of Prince Albert of Saxe-Coburg-Gotha, Queen Victoria's consort)

There is only one species in this genus, the Prince Albert's Yew (*Saxegothaea conspicua*) which is a native of Chile. It is an evergreen tree, yew-like in habit, attaining a height of 9 to 12 metres (30 to 40 feet) but differing from that tree by the curved leaves with white bands on the under surfaces. The fruit, too, looks more like that of the Juniper with

The Monkey Puzzle from Chile was a fashionable tree in Victorian Britain, and is still sometimes planted today.

The spiky, leathery leaves and the large, globular female cone of the Monkey Puzzle.

fleshy, grooved scales forming a sort of berry. The tree grows in dense forests on the lower mountain slopes but large specimens are too scarce to provide timber of any value.

Family Araucariaceae
GENUS *Araucaria*
(after the Araucani Indians of central Chile)

A genus of fifteen species of evergreen trees confined to the southern hemisphere. They have horizontal branches, usually in whorls, spirally arranged, scale-like, overlapping leaves of varying lengths up to 5 centimetres (2 inches), that are leathery and sharp pointed or awl-like. The male and female flowers are borne on separate trees and the cones are usually large and globular. The bark is thick and resinous, ridged and wrinkled round the old branch scars.

The best known species is the Monkey Puzzle (*Araucaria araucana*) or Chile Pine originating in Chile and the Argentine where it is found growing, sometimes to heights of 30 metres (100 feet), in the evergreen forests on the eastern slopes of the coastal mountain ranges, and often

Araucaria

The Norfolk Island Pine, remarkable for its symmetry, is a much-planted ornamental in subtropical countries.

at elevations of 1200 metres (4000 feet) or more. The stiff, broad, leathery and exceedingly sharp-pointed leaves invest the twigs in such a fashion that the Cornish owner of one of the first importations to Britain is reported to have told admiring friends that 'It would puzzle a monkey to climb the tree'. Hence the English name. A timber tree in its native lands, the Monkey Puzzle, which was discovered in 1795, became a very popular ornamental tree in Victorian times, and was much planted in suburban gardens where it is often seen to this day. Its popularity has waned over the years, but it still has a part to play in formal plantings, especially in groups. Young trees, furnished with branches right down to the ground are attractive curiosities, and the old trees, which become flat topped and bare boled, have a certain dignity. The large, golden-brown, globular cones which crowd the topmost branches of the mature female trees produce, in their second year, huge seeds 38 millimetres (1½ inches) long and edible when roasted.

The other South American araucaria, the Pirana Pine (*Araucaria angustifolia*) or Candelabra Tree, is native of hilly country in south Brazil, extending into Argentina. It grows to a height of 36 metres (120 feet) with a branch-free trunk topped by candelabra-like heads of upturned branches forming flattened crowns. The leaves are softer and more loosely arranged than in the Monkey Puzzle Tree. The tree produces the most important timber in Brazil and one which is in increasing demand in many countries for panelling. It is not as hardy as the Monkey Puzzle.

The Australian Hoop Pine (*Araucaria cunninghamii*) is a large tree generally attaining 30 to 45 metres (100 to 150 feet) in height but sometimes as much as 60 metres (200 feet). It occurs between sea-level and 600 metres (2000 feet) in the subtropical areas of south-east Queensland. The bole of the mature tree is free of branches and straight, with very little taper, and the leaves short and sharp barely more than 6·5 millimetres (¼ inch) long. The wood is excellent for indoor work and the tree is extensively used for afforestation in Queensland. Another tree of similar range and appearance, but with bigger leaves, is the Bunya Pine (*Araucaria bidwillii*) which does not reach the same height as the Hoop Pine – 42 metres (140 feet) being about the limit – nor is it so widespread. It makes an attractive ornamental tree in mild climates, as does the Norfolk Island Pine (*Araucaria heterophylla*), a very beautiful tree, often 60 metres (200 feet) tall, a native of that island in the Pacific. Mature trees are of exceptional symmetry and are planted extensively in many subtropical countries as ornamentals. Young trees, with their distinctive, soft, awl-like leaves are often grown as pot and greenhouse plants in temperate regions. The timber is as good as that of other members of the genus, but is much too scarce for commercial use.

The massive trunk of the New Zealand Kauri Pine shows its age to be about 1000 years.

GENUS *Agathis* kauris
(*agathis*, a ball of thread, referring to the round cone)

A genus of some twenty tall, evergreen, resinous trees confined to New Zealand, Australia, Malaysia, and some Pacific Islands. They have large, leathery, broad leaves with stalks, big globular cones, and massive columnar trunks covered with scaly bark from which gum resin exudes.

The Kauri (*Agathis australis*) is the noblest of New Zealand's trees, held in as much reverence in its native land as is the Redwood in America. It is confined naturally to the Auckland Province of North Island where it grows 45 metres (150 feet) tall with girths of 15 metres (50 feet) and more and clean boles with scarcely a taper for as much as 18 metres (60 feet). The area of crown spread is immense and the Kauri forest has an open appearance with the massive trunks seemingly supporting a vast, vaulted roof as pillars. With such quantities of first-rate timber in each tree – timber which has probably been 1000 years and more growing – it is not surprising that much devastation has been wrought among these trees by ruthless exploitation, so that very big trees are now rare. The gum resin which exudes from the bark and branches when wounded was also highly prized. Huge accumulated quantities of it were dug up from beneath the trees (some 15 000 tonnes annually) and when this semi-fossilized source was exhausted the trees were deliberately wounded with cuts to produce up to 23 kilograms (50 pounds) a year per tree. This digging and bleeding devastated the forests further. The last of the big Kauris are now confined to the Waipoua State Forest, 240 kilometres (150 miles) north of Auckland, but, such is the tree's reputation, it is planted throughout the country and many handsome specimens can be found in the milder districts.

A very similar tree, the South Queensland Kauri (*Agathis robusta*), has a very limited range in the south-east of that state and on Fraser Island, and two other species are found further north. A tropical species, the Mountain Agathis (*Agathis alba*), grows in Malaysia and Indonesia reaching huge dimensions and producing useful timber as well as gum.

The broad, leathery, evergreen leaves of the Kauri.

33

Family Cupressaceae
GENUS *Calocedrus* incense cedars
(*kalos*, beautiful, and *cedrus*, cedar)

A genus of large evergreen trees with aromatic, scale-like leaves, closely pressed and overlapping. The cones are small, leathery, and shaped like vases. They are found in north-west America, China, Taiwan, and New Zealand.

The best known is the north-west American Incense Cedar (*Calocedrus decurrens*) which is found south from Oregon along the western slopes of the Cascade and Sierra Nevada ranges into lower California, usually at altitudes between 900 and 2400 metres (3000 and 8000 feet). The tree is broadly pyramidal in its native range, but when planted in Europe or even in the eastern states of North America, it develops a narrow, columnar habit for reasons which are as yet unexplained. This singular shape, combined with its dark green, feathery foliage, make the tree a valuable addition to larger gardens and parks in Europe where it can reach heights of around 27 metres (90 feet). In north-west America

Calocedrus

heights of 45 metres (150 feet) are common, and one tree in Oregon is reported to be 67·5 metres (225 feet) tall. The timber is light brown in colour, light in weight, durable and aromatic, and is widely used for outdoor work such as fencing and telegraph poles, as well as for chests, pencils, and cigar boxes.

The Chilean Incense Cedar (*Calocedrus chilensis*) placed by some botanists in a separate genus, *Austrocedrus*, is a much smaller tree, about 15 metres (50 feet) tall, and a native of the lower slopes of the Andes in southern Chile, on rocky sites where few other trees can survive; it has not been a success in Europe, however. The Chinese species, *Calocedrus macrolepis*, is again a bigger tree, sometimes 30 metres (100 feet) tall, and a valuable timber tree in that country, but not hardy in Europe. Likewise, the two New Zealand species, the Pahautea (*Calocedrus bidwillii*) and the Kawaka (*Calocedrus plumosa*) are tender trees, although reaching 30 metres (100 feet) in the North Island and producing useful timber.

GENUS *Chamaecyparis* false cypresses
(*chamai*, dwarf and *kuparissos*, cypress – an inapt name)

A genus of six tall, pyramidal, evergreen trees with leaves in flattened, feathery sprays and small round cones with spikes like the head of a traditional ogre's club.

Although it is the most limited in natural distribution [a 210-kilometre (130-mile) stretch along the Pacific coast on the Oregon/Californian border] the Lawson Cypress (*Chamaecyparis lawsoniana*) or Port Orford Cedar is by far the best known and widespread member of this genus. The type tree, which is handsome enough itself and can grow to 60 metres (200 feet) in its native country, has, since its discovery in 1854 and its first planting in Lawson's nursery in Edinburgh, produced no less than seventy varieties or cultivars: large and small, thin and tall, light green and dark green, blue and gold. No other tree in the world has such variety. To describe them all is impossible but some of the better known are: the cultivars 'Allumii' – blue and columnar, 'Triomphe de Boskoop' – glaucous and broadly columnar, 'Lutea' – golden yellow and columnar with pendulous foliage, and 'Pottenii' – extremely narrow columnar with dense, pale-green, feathery foliage.

The long, scale-like leaves and the pointed, vase-shaped cone of the Incense Cedar.

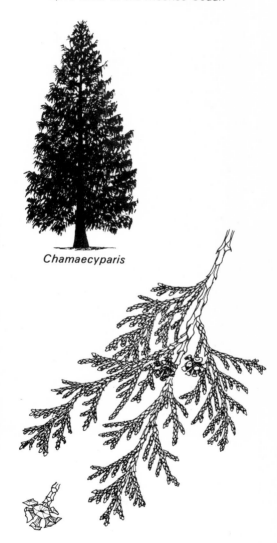

Chamaecyparis

The flattened, scale-like leaves and the round cone (here opened) of the Lawson Cypress.

Far left
A group of Incense Cedars showing the very narrow habit characteristic of these trees when growing in Europe.

Left
The round cones and the scale-like leaves of the Lawson Cypress.

35

Below
The golden variety of the Lawson Cypress is a fine subject for landscape planting.
Right
A Lawson Cypress hedge is neat, effective, and easily maintained.
Bottom
The Nootka Cypress is a graceful and symmetrical tree.

The type tree and some of the cultivars will stand clipping well and make excellent hedges.

The second of the trio of American false cypresses, the Nootka Cypress (*Chamaecyparis nootkatensis*) or Alaska Yellow Cedar is much less well known than the Lawson but with a much greater natural distribution stretching from southern Alaska, through British Columbia to Oregon. It is a medium-sized tree, rarely more than 24 metres (80 feet) tall, but very graceful and remarkably regular in shape. The foliage is medium green, hanging in arched, pendulous sprays and, like the Lawson, the tree is exceedingly hardy and tolerant of most soil conditions. The third species is the Atlantic White Cedar (*Chamaecyparis thyoides*) a tree of the eastern coastal regions of North America. From southern Maine to south-eastern Mississippi it grows almost entirely in fresh-water swamps and along river banks in very dense stands. In the south the tree may reach 24 metres (80 feet) in height, but in the north it rarely exceeds 15 metres (50 feet). It is very slow growing and not often seen in Europe.

One of the two Japanese species, the Hinoki Cypress (*Chamaecyparis obtusa*), is the only member of the genus with blunt, scale-like leaves. It is a graceful, pyramidal tree reaching heights of 30 to 36 metres (100 to 120 feet) in extensive forests in the south of Honshu. The timber is one of the best produced by coniferous trees and is employed extensively for building and many other uses in Japan. There is a number of cultivars including dwarfs, and the tree is much used in Japan for bonzai work. The other species indigenous to Japan and with the same range as the Hinoki but found on damper ground is the Sawara Cypress (*Chamaecyparis pisifera*) in which the leaf scales have fine, incurved points. This tree,

Above
The compact, dense foliage of the Hinoki Cypress; a fine specimen growing at Stourhead, Wiltshire, England.

Left
The golden form of the Hinoki Cypress, cultivar 'Crippsii', is very slow growing and often planted in small gardens.

Leyland Cypresses at Kyloe, Northumberland, England, grown from cuttings taken in 1898 from the original trees.

too, grows to 30 metres (100 feet) and more and produces good timber, but both in Japan and abroad is less well-known than its many cultivars grown mainly for their peculiarity of continuing to produce juvenile foliage even when mature.

The Formosan Cypress (*Chamaecyparis formosensis*) is very like the Sawara and reaches enormous sizes on Taiwan in forests between 2100 and 3000 metres (7000 and 10 000 feet) in company with the Hinoki. A tree measured at the beginning of the 1900s was 49.4 metres (162 feet) tall and 18 metres (60 feet) in girth, and trees of 59 metres (195 feet) have been reported, which make this the tallest of the genus; yet in Europe it never exceeds 15 metres (50 feet).

GENUS X *Cupressocyparis* hybrid cypresses

Three intergenetic crosses between false cypresses, *Chamaecyparis*, and the true cypresses, *Cupressus*, have occurred spontaneously in Britain; two so recently that little is known about the resulting hybrids.

In 1888, at Leighton Park, near Welshpool, seed from cones picked off a Nootka Cypress produced six seedlings which subsequently turned out to be hybrids between that cypress and a nearby Monterey Cypress (*Cupressus macrocarpa*). These were named Leyland Cypress (*Cupressocyparis leylandii*) after Captain Leyland who grew them. And these six trees, and some others resulting from a further cross in 1911 at the same place, but with the Monterey Cypress as the mother, have been the original source of nearly all the Leyland Cypresses in the world today. It is a tree which combines the qualities of quick growth of one of its parents with those of hardiness and adaptability of the other, and the grace of both. It forms narrow, green columns of varying hues according

The Monterey Cypress in its natural habitat—Poit Lobos, Monterey, California.

to the clone, and it does it very quickly–27 metres (90 feet) in fifty years is recorded for some of the early trees and an annual growth of 0·9 metre (3 feet) is quite usual in young trees. It is, then, an excellent tree to give quick results in a garden; and it forms evergreen hedges and screens in record time.

The other two hybrids occurred between the Smooth Arizona Cypress (*Cupressus glabra*) and the Nootka Cypress in 1956, also at Leighton, and between the Nootka Cypress again and the Mexican Cypress (*Cupressus lusitanica*) in 1961, at Westonbirt in Gloucestershire. Little is yet known about them and neither so far has an English name.

GENUS *Cupressus* true cypresses
(the latin name for the Italian Cypress)

A genus of some twenty species of evergreen trees found in south-west North America, the Mediterranean area and north Africa, the Himalayas, and China. The leaves are small and scale-like arranged closely around the shoots which are not flattened like the false cypresses. The cones, too, are much bigger and sometimes stay on the tree for years after dropping their seeds.

The Monterey Cypress (*Cupressus macrocarpa*) is a tree with a remarkably limited natural range, restricted to a small, windswept peninsula south of Monterey Bay in California. Nevertheless, it is a highly successful tree in many parts of the world where in youth it is narrow and erect, and somewhat cedar-like when old. The wild trees are mostly gnarled and misshapen and scarcely 18 metres (60 feet) tall. But trees grown in Britain and elsewhere have exceeded 30 metres (100 feet). Its coastal origin gives this cypress a resistance to salt winds and it

The small, closely arranged leaves and the circular cone of the Monterey Cypress.

is often planted in seaside gardens, particularly as hedges. This cypress, too, has produced a number of cultivars of which perhaps the most beautiful is a yellow one called 'Donard Gold'.

Of the other North American species, the Arizona Cypress [*Cupressus glabra (arizonica)*] is a very handsome tree. Found in southern Arizona and northern Mexico on mountain slopes and the sides of canyons, it grows to heights of about 21 metres (70 feet). The leaf scales which are greyish green are very small and compact, making the twigs tough and wiry. The bark is reddish brown and the whole tree is narrow, dense, and conical. A cultivar, 'Pyramidalis' is a bright, silvery blue and an excellent ornamental tree, often seen in towns and cities in many parts of the world. The remaining North American species, all very similar in appearance, are of little economic or amenity value except perhaps the Mexican Cypress (*Cupressus lusitanica*) a tree so long established in Portugal as to have been considered indigenous there, hence the scientific name; but there is no doubt that its real home is Mexico and south to the high mountains of Guatemala. A blue cultivar 'Glauca' makes an attractive tree in milder climates.

The Italian Cypress (*Cupressus sempervirens*), sometimes called the Mediterranean Cypress, extends throughout that region, north to Switzerland and east to Persia. It is that tall, narrow, dark-green tree so often seen on the barren white, rocky slopes which dip into the blue Mediterranean or in little groups shading hillside villas. It is, indeed, the cypress of Roman times and probably a long-cultivated variety of the original type which tends to be more spreading. No tree is more typical of southern Europe.

Further east, in the Himalayas, there are two cypresses, the Kashmir Cypress (*Cupressus cashmeriana*), a rare and graceful tree of unknown natural origin but much planted in Kashmir, and the Bhutan Cypress (*Cupressus torulosa*) a large tree found in the eastern Himalayas and on into China, sometimes reaching over 30 metres (100 feet) in height and growing at elevations from 1500 to 2700 metres (5000 to 9000 feet). In China, too, is the Weeping Cypress (*Cupressus funebris*), its ascending branches ending in long, pendulous, slender branchlets.

Above
The blue variety of the Arizona Cypress is an exceptionally handsome conifer.

Right
Spire-like Italian Cypresses in the south of France.

GENUS *Fitzroya*
(after Admiral R Fitzroy who commanded H.M.S. *Beagle*)

A genus with a single species distinguished by its scale-like leaves set in threes, hard, thick and blunt, and only about 3 mm (1¼ inches) long. The cones, too, have three whorls of three scales each.

The sole representative is the Alerce (*Fitzroya cupressoides*) or Patagonian Cypress, rarely heard of in the northern hemisphere but one of the elite of temperate conifers rivalling the redwoods for longevity and quality of timber. It is also a tree of considerable stature reaching 48 metres (160 feet) in height and some 9 metres (30 feet) in girth, growing in pure stands on mountain slopes at 600 to 900 metres (2000 to 3000 feet) in a fairly restricted area of southern Chile. The timber has been worked for many centuries and the more accessible stands had already been worked out when Darwin, in H.M.S. *Beagle* visited the area in 1833. The remoter stands are still being worked, but the Chilean government has established a national park to preserve some of the older stands which have escaped the axe.

GENUS *Juniperus* junipers
(the old Latin name for the tree)

A genus of some sixty species of evergreen trees ranging over most of the northern hemisphere from the Arctic Circle to the tropics. They differ from other members of the Cupressaceae in their fleshy cone scales uniting to form what looks like a berry. Their leaves are of two kinds: sharp, awl-shaped, and standing out from the twig; or scale-like and pressed close to the twig. Some species bear both kinds of leaves, and all of them have the awl-shaped type when seedlings.

The Common Juniper (*Juniperus communis*) has a wider natural distribution than any other tree in the world. It is found throughout Europe and eastwards through Asia Minor, Iran, Afghanistan, and the western Himalayas, and in North America. It is a small tree, even a shrub in many places, rarely exceeding 12 metres (40 feet), the type being well known only because its berries are used for flavouring gin.

A group of Common Junipers growing in Dumfries, Scotland.

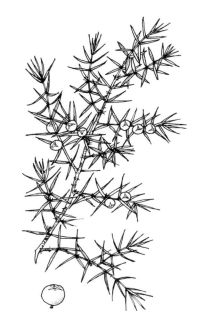

The sharp, awl-shaped leaves and the berry-like fruits of the Common Juniper.

The Chinese Juniper is a narrow, symmetrical tree, especially in middle age.

Its numerous cultivars, especially the dense columnar 'Stricta' and the flame-shaped 'Suecica' have made it a favourite with gardeners.

The American Pencil Cedar (*Juniperus virginiana*) is a much bigger tree, sometimes as tall as 30 metres (100 feet) in the alluvial soils in the southern part of its huge eastern North American range, stretching from Quebec to Texas. As the name implies, the timber of this tree is preferred above all others for making pencils. It, too, has a large number of cultivars. The Sierra Juniper (*Juniperus occidentalis*) is a mountain species from north-west America which attains considerable girth, up to 2·7 metres (9 feet) but not the height of the Pencil Cedar, as it clings to rocky mountain sides; and another species, even more spartan in its requirements, is the Desert Juniper (*Juniperus utahensis*) which grows extensively on sites which would otherwise be devoid of trees – sandy soils on desert foothills and mountain slopes between 1500 and 2400 metres (5000 and 8000 feet) in Utah and surrounding states. From Arizona and New Mexico comes the Alligator Juniper (*Juniperus pachyphloea*) remarkable for its thick bark divided into scaly squares resembling the skin of an alligator, a feature helping its high resistance to drought, much prevelant in its native parts.

Of the European and Near Eastern junipers, an interesting species is the Syrian Juniper (*Juniperus drupaceae*), also found growing to heights of 12 metres (40 feet) in Greece and Asia Minor. It has the biggest awl-shaped leaves of the whole genus, and also the biggest fruit, up to 25·4 millimetres (1 inch) in diameter and said to be edible. The Phoenician Juniper (*Juniperus phoenicea*), a small tree up to 12 metres (40 feet) tall, is common throughout the Mediterranean region, north Africa, and the Canary Islands where it attains its greatest size and age. In Algeria it is often the only tree in mountainous areas up to 1800 metres (6000 feet).

The East African Juniper (*Juniperus procera*) is a forest tree up to 36 metres (120 feet) tall and 9 metres (30 feet) in girth found in the east African highlands between 2100 and 2700 metres (7000 and 9000 feet). It produces a valuable, fragrant, and even-grained timber much used for building and furniture. Efforts at large-scale afforestation with this tree within its natural range have been abandoned because of its slow growth and its tendency to produce fluted trunks.

From the Himalayas and Burma comes the Drooping Juniper (*Juniperus recurva*), a tree of graceful, weeping habit found growing up to 12 metres (40 feet) tall in the moist, sheltered valleys of Sikkim and upper Burma where it attains its best development, and even up to 3600 metres (12 000 feet) where it is smaller but often the only tree able to survive. The other Himalayan species the Black Juniper (*Juniperus wallichiana*) extends over the whole great mountain range from the Indus to Bhutan and is a bigger tree than its drooping relative, reaching 18 metres (60 feet).

The Chinese Juniper (*Juniperus chinensis*), which is also indigenous in Japan, is very variable in habit, sometimes a large tree 18 metres (60 feet) tall and sometimes shrubby or even prostrate. It is particularly popular in Japan as an ornamental tree and is often planted near temples and in gardens. It also produces a large number of cultivars and, again in Japan, is much used for bonzai work.

The graceful, weeping habit of the Drooping Juniper is displayed well in this photograph.

Above
When open-grown on a lawn, the Western Red Cedar spreads out from the base to form a broad cone.

Below
The leaves of the Hiba are silvery white beneath and the cones are rounder than the Red Cedar's.

GENUS *Thuya* arbor vitae
(from the Greek *thuia*, a resin-bearing tree)

A genus of six large, evergreen, cypress-like trees from North America, China, Japan, and Taiwan. They differ from the cypresses in their urn-shaped cones with thin scales, and in their scale-like leaves being broader and larger.

The best-known species is the Western Red Cedar (*Thuya plicata*) which is a huge tree, often 60 metres (200 feet) tall, widely distributed in the Pacific coastal strip of north-west America. It is one of the conifer giants which form the unique forests of that area. The heavily buttressed trunks, sometimes as much as 15 metres (50 feet) in girth near the ground, produce a very valuable timber known the world over for its unusual resistance to insect and fungal attack. It may be used unpainted for roof shingles, building, and for greenhouses. Open grown, the tree makes a handsome ornamental, and the cultivar 'Zebrina' has green and gold bands on the foliage, giving it an attractive pepper-and-salt colour. The other American species, the White Cedar (*Thuya occidentalis*) which ranges across eastern and central Canada and southwards through the Appalachian Mountains, is a less impressive tree and much less tall than the Red Cedar, usually only about 18 metres (60 feet). The timber is also very durable but has never been available in the huge sizes of the Red Cedar and many of the large stands have long since worked out. This tree bears cones at a very early age, and quite small trees are often turned reddish brown all over by a solid mass of cones. A cultivar, 'Rheingold', popular in small gardens, is a small, golden bush bearing the feathery juvenile foliage.

The Japanese Thuya (*Thuya standishii*) grows to some 18 metres (60 feet) in hilly areas of central Japan and has silvery green shoots, whereas the Chinese Thuya (*Thuya orientalis*) from the north of that country and Korea, is a small, gaunt, upright tree with dark-green foliage, unlike the true Korean Thuya (*Thuya koraiensis*) which has white undersides to its leaf scales. None of these oriental thuyas produces timber of any great value.

GENUS *Thuyopsis*
(resembling *Thuya*)

A genus of one species closely allied to the thuyas but with larger leaves that are silvery underneath and rounder cones.

The Hiba (*Thuyopsis dolabrata*) is a large, evergreen tree up to 30 metres (100 feet) in height found throughout central and southern Japan where it is a very important timber tree. Some of the best forests in Japan are of this species situated on the peninsulas of Shimokita and Tsugaru in northern Honshu. It was one of five trees chosen for preservation in the mid-1500s when much attention was given to forest administration, and this may account for the fine forests mentioned above. The tree is also a favourite with Japanese gardeners. The timber is used for building and engineering work and also as a basis for lacquer work.

GENUS *Callitris* cypress pines
(from *kali*, beautiful, and *tri*, three, referring to leaf arrangement)

A genus of fourteen or so medium-sized, evergreen trees and shrubs, native to Australia, with minute, scale-leaves and round or pyramidal cones. They are well adapted to arid regions.

The White Cypress Pine (*Callitris glauca*), a tree attaining a height of 21 to 24 metres (70 to 80 feet) and a girth of 1·8 to 2·4 metres (6 to 8 feet), is the most widespread of the genus, occurring in extensive forests mixed with eucalypts in New South Wales and south Queensland and, in smaller dimensions, in scattered areas westwards as far as central Western Australia. It enjoys an inland, warm, temperate to subtropical climate and in areas where the rainfall is high [700 milli-metres (28 inches)] it can reach 30 metres (100 feet) in height. The timber is renowned for its resistance to decay and white ant attacks, and for its very small shrinkage when seasoned.

The Common Cypress Pine (*Callitris robusta*) is a tree of similar size and appearance as the white species (some say it is the same species) which grows extensively on dry sites in Western Australia. The timber has similar properties to that of the White Cypress Pine and

The wide, scale-like leaves and the small, urn-shaped cone of the Western Red Cedar.

The large, silvery, scale-like leaves and the round cone of the Hiba.

the tree is used as shelter for orchards in Western Australia.

In the extreme north of Australia the Northern Cypress Pine (*Callitris intratropica*) is the most important timber tree able to thrive in the very hot, dry climate but very liable to devastation by the forest fires which are frequent. This danger, combined with excessive cutting over the years, has rendered the larger trees, between 15 and 24 metres (50 and 80 feet) tall, in very short supply.

GENUS *Widdringtonia*
(after the botanist, Edward Widdrington)
A genus of five small to medium-sized, evergreen trees, confined to south and central Africa and closely related to the Australian cypress pine (*Callitris*) but differing from them in their smaller scale-leaves, arranged in pairs, and in their cones having four scales instead of six to eight.

The urn-shaped cones of the Western Red Cedar are opening to shed their seed.

The spirally arranged leaves and round, leathery cone of the Californian Coast Redwood.

The beautiful, soft, red bark of Coast Redwoods growing in a grove belonging to the Royal Forestry Society at Leighton, Welshpool, Wales.

The Clanwilliam Cedar (*Widdringtonia juniperoides*) is a fairly large tree up to 18 metres (60 feet) in height and 3 metres (10 feet) in diameter, found only on the Cedarberg mountains in the Clanwilliam District, the trees scattered or in clumps. Formerly, it formed much of the forest which covered the mountains up to 6000 feet but fire and ruthless exploitation have worked terrible destruction and the giant trees, whose stumps were still there at the turn of the century, suggesting girths of 7·5 to 9 metres (25 to 30 feet), are now nowhere to be found. But the timber is still the most valuable in South Africa and is used for high quality furniture. The other member of the genus which reaches a reasonable size is the Willowmore Cedar (*Widdringtonia schwarzii*) found in mountains 560 kilometres (350 miles) east of the Cedarberg in some of the most spectacular scenery in South Africa. Practically all the accessible trees have disappeared, and mature specimens are only to be found in steep gorges. Here, the trees can be up to 24 metres (80 feet) tall, and one was reported to have reached 29 metres (96 feet). Restricted though these trees now are, they still seem to be regenerating naturally; more so than the Clanwilliam Cedar, although the saplings are cut in large numbers for the framework of native huts.

The Mlanji Cedar (*Widdringtonia whytei*) is a large tree up to 42 metres (140 feet) in height and 4·5 metres (15 feet) in girth, which grows at 1800 metres (6000 feet) to 2100 metres (7000 feet) on Mount Mlanji in southern Malawi and southwards into Rhodesia and the northern Transvaal. The existing forests were once much more extensive but this species, like all the genus, is highly inflammable and huge areas have been destroyed by fire, making the timber, though valuable, too scarce except for local use. The juvenile foliage is very attractive and the tree is used as a substitute for the more traditional Christmas tree in central Africa.

Family Taxodiaceae

GENUS *Sequoia*
(after a half-caste Indian Sequoiah who invented the Cherokie alphabet)

A genus of one species of giant, evergreen trees with scale-like leaves on the leading and cone-bearing shoots, and spirally set needles that are dark green, with two white bands on the underside, on the laterals. The 25-millimetre (1-inch) long cones have wrinkled, leathery scales. The bark is soft, thick, and russet.

The Californian Coast Redwood (*Sequoia sempervirens*) is one of the world's most famous and impressive trees; it is also the tallest. The 'Howard Libbey' tree discovered about ten years ago, is 110 metres (367 feet) tall, and there are many Redwoods in the national parks well over 90 metres (300 feet). They are confined to a narrow Pacific coastal strip, stretching from the Canadian border to southern California with their finest development in the northern part of that state. Here, on the coastal flats, with constant sea fogs providing just the right humidity, the almost pure forests of these trees are quite magnificent. Enormous, heavily buttressed, towering trunks, clear of branches for 45 metres (150 feet) and more are densely grouped together like red pillars supporting the green roof of some vast building. The trees are not only of great size, they are also of great age. Many of them in such a stand will be 400 to 800 years old, with here and there veterans of over 2000 years. One factor which enables these trees to live so long, apart from their unusual resistance to wood-rotting fungi, is the immensely thick bark [0·3 metre (1 foot) thick in large trees] which protects them from forest fires – a real threat in any forest over a period of two millennia. Such closely growing stands would not be perpetuated unless the Redwoods had another characteristic, rare in conifers, the ability to reproduce themselves from sprouts which spring up from the stumps. Circles of young trees can be seen growing round the rim of an old stump with a vigour which gives them a better start than seedlings.

The earliest recorded discovery of the Redwoods was in 1769 when a Father Crespi, the recorder of a Spanish expedition noted that the coastal plains and low hills around the shores of Monterey Bay were 'well forested with very high trees of a red colour, not known to us'. He named them *Palo Colorado* (red tree) which, in effect, is the name Redwood in use today.

The exploitation of the Redwood timber since the beginning of this century has been enormous and extremely damaging to the forests. It was only in the 1930s that steps were taken to preserve some of the best remaining stands and these are now made safe in a number of parks, some of 4000 hectares (10 000 acres) and more, astride the famous Californian Highway 101. Few finer stands of trees can be seen anywhere else in the world.

A Coast Redwood, 100 metres (329 feet) tall, growing at Big Basin, California and known as the 'Father of the Forest'.

47

The sharp-pointed, scale-like leaves and the large, round cone of the Wellingtonia.

GENUS *Sequoiadendron*
(from *Sequoia* (q.v.) and *dendron*, tree)

A genus of one species of mammoth, evergreen trees closely related to the Redwoods but differing from them in having sharp-pointed, scale-like leaves, spirally arranged and adhering to the branches, and with larger cones 75 millimetres (3 inches) long.

The Wellingtonia (US Sequoia) (*Sequoiadendron giganteum*) or Big Tree, or Sierra Redwood is the biggest tree in the world. Some of the old trees still standing are over 80 metres (260 feet) tall with girths of nearly 24 metres (80 feet) above the buttressed bases. Such trees are estimated to weigh more than 2000 tonnes. A tree felled some years ago was reported to be 110 metres (365 feet) tall, and ring counts on felled trees of 80 metres (260 feet) or so reveal an age of between 1200 and 2000 years. The stump of one tree recorded 3400 rings and another with over 4000 is recorded. There is no doubt that the Wellingtonia is a very long liver, standing for many hundreds of years as a massive example of the supreme achievement of plant creation.

These trees, in the wild state, are now restricted to seventy-two groves of from five to 1000 trees each on the western slopes of the Sierra Nevada in California at heights of between 1200 and 2400 metres (4000 and 8000 feet). These groves are an awe-inspiring sight. Although the

Above
The Japanese Cedar, with its varying greens and yellows, makes a handsome ornamental tree.

Right
The red, shaggy bark of a Summit Cedar in Cornwall, England.

trees are more spaced out than the Redwoods, the huge cinnamon-red trunks supported on enormous buttressed roots, tower up without a branch for 60 metres (200 feet) and more in such overwhelming bulk as to defy the imagination and to cast doubts as to their being living things. Yet high above are the thick, green crowns, somewhat thin in the ancients, and below are the attendant pines and firs, great trees in their own rights, but dwarfed by the giants. Young Wellingtonias in the groves are very scarce. The thick carpet of leaf litter and the trampling of tourists which compacts the soil inhibit the growth of any seedlings let alone those of the Wellingtonias which in the best of circumstances are poor reproducers. Statistics show that only one seed in a million is likely to germinate under natural conditions and only a small percentage of these survive. In the prepared soil of forest nurseries Wellingtonia seedlings are easily grown, however, and the groves can be perpetuated by planting.

Like the Redwoods, the Wellingtonias are immune to most diseases and are threatened only by fire, but with their bark up to 0·6 metre (two feet) thick few have succumbed to this hazard although serious forest fires are likely to occur at least three times in a century. Nor do gales worry them; their immense buttressed bases give them sure stability. And their timber, which is light, rather brittle, and of little use, has saved them from the axe. We are still able to enjoy trees which have stood for a thousand years. Their offspring, since the first seeds were sent to Britain in 1846, have been planted all over the temperate world and some of them, although only one tenth the age of their elders, are already trees of majestic proportions.

GENUS *Cryptomeria*
(from *krypto*, to hide, *meris*, a part, referring to hidden flowers)

A genus of one species of large, evergreen trees resembling the *Sequoiadendron* but differing from it in having leaves less closely adhering to the branches and in five ranks instead of three. The bark, too, is much thinner and becomes detached in long shreds.

The Japanese Cedar (*Cryptomeria japonica*) is a large tree up to 45 metres (150 feet) tall and 7·5 metres (25 feet) in girth found growing in extensive forests in central Japan, where it is the most important timber tree, and in China. The tall, tapering stems clad in reddish bark form stands rivalling the Redwoods in California. Cryptomerias, too, can live to a great age and some giant trees in Japan are 1000 years old, designated as national monuments because this species, too, like the Hiba, has been protected since the 1500s. In addition to its widespread use for afforestation in Japan and many other countries, and its universally useful timber, the Cryptomeria is much loved by the Japanese as an ornamental tree; grouped around temples, planted in avenues and in groves, this tree contributes much to the charm of the urban scene in that country. It also has many cultivars: 'Lobbii' which has longer, denser, and more compact leaves, and 'Elegans' which is bushy and turns brown in the autumn, are two of the more common cultivars of the Japanese Cedar.

GENUS *Athrotaxis* Tasmanian cedars
(*athroos*, crowded, *taxis*, arrangements, referring to the leaves)

A genus of three very similar species of evergreen trees confined to western Tasmania, with spirally arranged, scale-like leaves, small, round, woody cones, and slightly furrowed bark, peeling in shreds.

The tallest is the King William Pine (*Athrotaxis selaginoides*) a gaunt, medium-sized tree reaching 24 to 27 metres (80 to 90 feet) in height in steep, broken country and on exposed ridge tops up to 900 metres (3000 feet). It occurs in small stands and is very slow growing so that mature specimens are now rare. The timber is good, resembling in many respects that of the Californian Redwoods, soft and straight grained.

The other two species are lesser trees with smaller, more closely pressed leaves. They are the Smooth Tasmanian Cedar (*Athrotaxis cupressoides*) which has rounded shoots with very closely pressed leaf scales, and grows to about 12 metres (40 feet) and the Summit Cedar (*Athrotaxis laxifolia*) with slightly bigger leaves, pale yellow when young, which only grows to 9 metres (30 feet) and at high elevations.

The forward-curving, pointed leaves and the spiny round cone of the Japanese Cedar.

The spirally arranged, scale-like leaves and the round cones, opened to shed their seed, of the Summit Cedar.

GENUS *Cunninghamia*
(after James Cunningham, an East India Company surgeon and botanist)

A genus of two large, evergreen trees, native to China and Taiwan with leaves resembling the Monkey Puzzle, but smaller and narrower, and with cones much smaller, bearing three seeds on each scale, instead of one.

The Chinese Fir (*Cunninghamia lanceolata*) is widely distributed in the mountains of central and southern China where it reaches 45 metres (150 feet) in height with a mast-like trunk free of branches for half of its length. Like the Redwood, it sprouts from the base when cut and in this way regenerates itself in areas where seeding might fail. The best of the fragrant timber is used for coffin boards, for which high prices are paid, but the timber generally is much in demand and is the most useful, apart from bamboo, for all-round work in China. The other much rarer species, *Cunninghamia konishii*, found only in Taiwan, has smaller, spirally arranged leaves, but it is very similar in appearance.

Above
The leaves of the Chinese Fir resemble those of the Monkey Puzzle but are smaller and softer.

Right
Although it is happy in or out of water, the Swamp Cypress looks its best when growing at the water's edge.

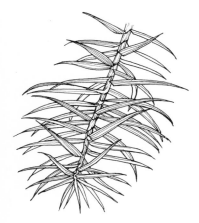

The pointed, stalkless leaves of the Chinese Fir.

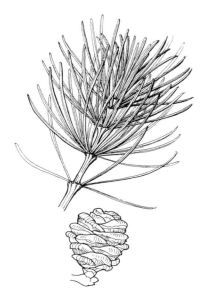

The whorls of needles, fused in pairs, and the round, loosely scaled cones of the Japanese Umbrella Pine.

GENUS *Sciadopitys*
(*skiados*, an umbel, *pitys*, a pine tree)

A genus with a single species of large evergreen trees easily distinguished by their 125-millimetre (5-inch) long, narrow leaves which are fused in pairs and arranged in whorls round the branches like the ribs of an umbrella. The round cones, 75 millimetres (3 inches) long, have loose, flexible scales.

The Japanese Umbrella Pine (*Sciadopitys verticillata*) reaches 30 metres (100 feet) in height and is found sporadically in steep, rocky, sheltered situations in central Japan at elevations up to 900 metres (3000 feet), growing with cypresses and firs. The timber is very durable in water and is used for boat building and bath tubs, and the fibrous bark is used for caulking and insulation. The tree is popular as an ornamental both in Japan and many other countries because of its unique leaf arrangement and its well-furnished habit when young.

GENUS *Taxodium* swamp cypresses
(*taxus*, yew, *eidios*, resembling)

A genus of three closely related, large deciduous trees, confined to southern North America and Mexico, with soft, pale-green leaves in two flattened ranks on shoots which are also shed in autumn. The winter buds are small, round, and scaly, the cones are round with shield-like scales, and the bark is red and ridged, peeling off in strips.

The Swamp Cypress (*Taxodium distichum*) is a tree, often up to 39 metres (130 feet) tall, which is equally happy on land or in water. From Florida through the Gulf States to Mexico it stands on a massive buttressed trunk, with curious, cone-shaped 'knees' through which it breathes, rising from the roots above the stagnant water, bearing a

The soft leaves on deciduous, alternate side shoots and the globular cone of the Swamp Cypress.

The Japanese Umbrella Pine has leaves arranged in whorls like the spines of an opened umbrella.

Taxodium

The soft leaves on deciduous, opposite side shoots, and the ovoid cone of the Dawn Redwood.

54

spreading crown, often festooned with mosses. It is one of the most beautiful conifers, particularly in spring, when the feathery leaves flush pale green, and again in the autumn when the leaves turn a deep reddish brown before falling. In swampy areas these trees form pure stands, but elsewhere they are mixed with other species. In Tertiary times similar trees were spread throughout North America and northern Europe but the Swamp Cypress is the sole survivor of this ancient family. The durable timber is easily worked and has many uses.

Another species, the Pond Cypress (*Taxodium ascendens*), is a smaller, more slender tree growing in more or less the same area, with small, scale-like leaves pressed along the shoots which rise vertically from the branches.

The Mexican Cypress (*Taxodium mucronatum*) is nearly evergreen, only casting its leaves all at one time when planted outside its natural range, the high tableland of Mexico south into Guatemala. Several immense specimens of this tree are known; one called *El Gigante*, growing near the church at Tule, is 35 metres (115 feet) in girth and 42 metres (140 feet) tall.

Of another and very similar genus is the Chinese Swamp Cypress (*Glyptostobus lineatus*), a small tree differing from the taxodiums in that its leaves are arranged in three ranks instead of two and its cones being egg shaped rather than round. It is of no economic importance.

GENUS *Metasequoia*
(*meta*, changing, *sequoia*, redwood)

A fascinating remnant genus of one species of large deciduous trees thought to be extinct since Pliocene times, when they covered much of the world, but discovered growing in China in 1941. They closely resemble the Swamp Cypresses but the branches and leaves are opposite and not alternate and the boles are often enlarged and fluted at the base.

The Dawn Redwood (*Metasequoia glyptostroboides*) like the Ginkgo, is a living fossil but one discovered only thirty-five years ago when a Chinese botanist found a hundred or so large specimens, and later a thousand more, some of them small and planted by man, in the Shui-sha valley of Hupeh Province. It is remarkable that a tree long known to the local people and used by them for feeding animals should have escaped the notice of the great plant collectors of the 1800s. Seeds were collected and widely distributed in 1948 and the tree is now quite common in many countries, where its quick growth [up to 1 metre (3 feet) a year when young] its slender elegance, and its beautiful foliage, bright green in spring and brick red in autumn, have made it a valuable ornamental tree. It stands cold winters but likes a warm summer for rapid growth. Although cones have appeared on quite small trees, the male flowers have not yet been borne by trees in Europe; thus, there has so far been no viable seed but the tree is readily reproduced from cuttings. Its ultimate height growth outside China, its timber qualities, and its life span are all things which will not become apparent for many years. No other tree in the world presents us with such a fascinating prospect.

Family Pinaceae
GENUS *Abies* silver firs
(from *abise*, to rise – referring to height)

A genus of about fifty species of large, handsome, symmetrical, evergreen trees from the northern temperate regions of Europe, Asia, and North America. They differ from all other conifers in having disc-shaped leaf scars on the twigs, and upright cones which disintegrate as soon as the seeds are ripe. The leaves are rarely sharp pointed but are usually blunt and fairly soft.

Of the European firs, the Common Silver Fir (*Abies alba*) is the most widespread, found growing wild in the mountains of central and southern Europe. It attains its maximum size in the Jura Mountains – between 36 and 42 metres (120 and 140 feet) in height with clean boles of up to 24 metres (80 feet) that are grey, even white, in the sunshine. It is one of the most important forest trees in France, Switzerland, and Germany, producing a light, soft timber well suited for interior building work. Pure stands are found in some areas but the tree is more usually seen in mixture with beech and spruce.

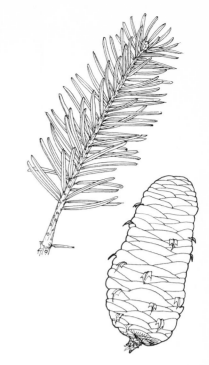

The upright female cone and a twig of the Common Silver Fir showing circular leaf scars typical of *Abies*.

Top left
Only discovered in 1941, the Dawn Redwood is now grown in all temperate countries; this is a young tree at Christchurch, New Zealand.

Bottom left
The bright-green, feathery leaves and the fluted bole of the Dawn Redwood.

Above
The silvery bark of the Common Silver Fir is one of its most attractive features.

The Caucasian Fir (*Abies nordmanniana*), which comes from the mountains to the south of the Black Sea and from the western spurs of the Caucasus, differs from the Common Silver Fir in being taller, some 60 metres (200 feet), and in having its leaves pointing forward along and over the top of the twig and not spreading each side, whereas the Cilician Fir (*Abies cilicica*) is a lesser tree with smaller, less-pointed leaves. The timber of both is locally important.

The Greek Fir (*Abies cephalonica*) has stiff, spiny leaves which radiate from all round the stem, with rather more above than below; while the Spanish Fir (*Abies pinsapo*) has even stiffer and sharper leaves radiating perpendicularly all round and out from the stem to the extent that the tree is often called the Hedgehog Fir. It has a very restricted range around Ronda in southern Spain and is about the only member of the genus which is happy on chalky soils. The Algerian Fir (*Abies numidica*) differs again in having its leaves very densely set and very short on the upper side of the shoots, those in the middle often pointing backwards.

In North America the silver firs reach their optimum development and are mostly giant trees in the north-west Pacific coastal belt. The Giant Fir (*Abies grandis*), found from the north of Vancouver Island south through Washington, Oregon, to California, reaches a height of 75 to 90 metres (250 to 300 feet) and is distinguished from all other firs by its long, notched leaves spread flat and comb-like on either side of the shoot. Twenty-five to 50 millimetres (1 to 2 inches) long, these leaves are shiny, slightly yellowish green above with two white lines on the underside. Striking though these huge firs are, their timber is of little use other than for pulp.

The Giant Fir may be the tallest but the Noble Fir (*Abies procera*), as its name implies, is the true aristocrat of the American firs. In its native forest, ranging from north Washington southwards along the Cascade Mountains to central Oregon, and growing at its best, it is a magnificent tree, lifting its crown on a clean and symmetrical trunk, sometimes as much as 7·5 metres (25 feet) in girth, 60 metres (200 feet) into the air. The curved leaves, varying in colour from pale to dark bluish green, appear to grow in a crowded mass along the upper sides of the branches and look quite different from those of the Giant Fir. The huge cones, up to 230

Abies

The sharp, stiff, spiky needles of the Spanish Fir resemble the spines of a hedgehog.

Left
The sharply pointed bracts protrude and bend downwards almost covering the scales of this Noble Fir cone.

Below
The upright-growing cones of the Giant Fir are typical of the genus *Abies*.

millimetres (9 inches) long, are distinct and differ from all other firs in having sharply pointed bracts which cover the scales like tiles on a roof; as in other firs they are borne upright on the topmost branches. The timber is of good quality and is much used for interior building work.

The Red Fir (*Abies magnifica*), a more mountainous species growing at between 2100 and 2700 metres (7000 and 9000 feet) in the Sierra Nevada where it attains heights of 53 metres (175 feet), has leaves very similar to the Noble Fir in form and colour, but they are longer, and rounder in section. The tree, too, looks different, being more conical and slender and the cones, although just as big, do not have the long bracts. Another very shapely species is the Beautiful Fir (*Abies amabilis*), which combines a narrow, conic habit with a striking, silvery whiteness to the undersides of the leaves which distinguish it from the Giant and Noble Firs in whose range it also grows to similar dimensions. The conspicuous purple cones are only about half the size of those of its two companions.

The slender spires of the Alpine Fir (*Abies lasiocarpa*) are a characteristic feature of large areas of mountainous country of western North America. From Alaska to the high ranges of British Columbia south to New Mexico and west into Montana and Idaho, this fir is the most widely distributed on the western side of the subcontinent. The largest specimens are found growing up to 45 metres (150 feet) tall at elevations of 1500 to 2400 metres (5000 to 8000 feet) in protected valleys and around mountain lakes, as well as of more modest sizes on rocky slopes at 3000 metres (10 000 feet) and more. The grey-green leaves, which rise forward along the shoot, have two white bands on the underside and one thin one on the top, particularly noticeable in the young growth giving it a silvery tinge. Another mountain species is the White Fir (*Abies concolor*) which grows at widely varying altitudes in an extensive range covering California, Nevada, Utah, and Arizona but attains its maximum development in northern California on north and east slopes at between 1200 and 1800 metres (4000 and 6000 feet) where it may be up to 60 metres (200 feet) tall. The leaves are stout, blunt pointed, and yellow-green in colour. The cones are green and, like those of all the true firs, they are held upright on the branches disintegrating in the autumn leaving woody spikes which remain on the branches for years.

All these north-west American firs grow well in Europe and elsewhere, and some of them are important timber trees in many parts of the world.

The Balsam Fir (*Abies balsamea*) is the species found in the cold, moist climate of south-east Canada and north-eastern United States, reaching eastwards as far as the Prairie provinces and westwards to Nova Scotia and the New England States. It is a tree of extraordinary arrowhead symmetry but small in comparison with the western species, attaining heights of only about 21 metres (70 feet). The deep blue-green aromatic leaves are arranged like a double comb either side of the shoot and the cones are cylindrical and about 200 millimetres (4 inches) long. The soft, brittle timber is quickly perishable and is mostly used for pulping. Its abundant resin, held in bark blisters, is the raw material of Canada balsam used in pharmacy. The other eastern American fir, Faser's Balsam Fir (*Abies fraseri*), found only on the highest peaks of the Alleghany Mountains from 1200 metres to 1800 metres (4000 to 6000 feet), is a small tree like its near relative but is distinguished from it by the young shoots being covered with reddish hair and the leaves being shorter and whiter beneath. Both the balsam firs, because of their symmetry, are popular as Christmas trees in America and Canada. Neither of them grows well in Europe.

The Santa Lucia Fir (*Abies bracteata*), with a very restricted range in the mountains of that name in Monterey County, California, is one of the most beautiful of the genus and also one of the rarest. Its conic shape with closely set branches, the topmost with hanging foliage and the lowest sweeping to the ground, make it a most handsome tree and a favourite, if rather rare, ornamental.

The Sacred Fir (*Abies religiosa*) is found in Central America from southern Mexico to Guatemala where it is a large tree up to 39 metres (130 feet) in height. The branches are much used for decorating places of worship at times of religious festivals and the cones are very beautiful, blue and seemingly spangled with gold, as the long, yellowish-brown bracts hang down over the scales.

The majority of the firs are native to Asia from the Himalayas through China to Japan. The West Himalayan Fir (*Abies pindrow*) is found from Afghanistan to Nepal and is a large tree up to 60 metres (200 feet) in height and 7·9 metres (26 feet) in girth, found growing in dense forests with other conifers on the great spurs of the mountains up to 3600 metres (12 000 feet). The leaves are long and hard with notched tips, and their irregular arrangement, together with the large, resinous buds, distinguish this tree from the East Himalayan Fir (*Abies specta-bilis*) which has much smaller buds, leaves intensely white beneath, and a wider crown. It also grows at higher elevations, and its range extends eastwards as far as Bhutan. Both trees produce white, straight-grained wood used locally for building purposes and general carpentry.

The Siberian Fir (*Abies sibirica*) is the most widespread of all the firs, its range extending right across Russia and Siberia and south to Turkestan and China. It rarely attains a height of more than 30 metres (100 feet), but is a classically conical tree, its drooping branches holding flat plates of light-green leaves slightly upset on hairy twigs, which distinguish it from its near relative the Sakhalin Fir (*Abies sachalinensis*), which has darker-green foliage and a ribbed shoot, and is found in the Kurile Islands and in Hokkaido where it is one of the most important forest trees.

Four species of this genus are confined to Japan. In the lower-lying, warmer parts of central and southern Japan the Momi Fir (*Abies firma*) is one of the principal trees of the indigenous forests and grows up to 36 metres (120 feet) tall and differs from all the other firs in having leaves with two sharp points held on grooved shoots. The timber is pure white

Even when young, the Beautiful Fir, in Herefordshire, England, shows a typical conic symmetry.

and much in demand for many uses. On higher ground, the Nikko Fir (*Abies homolepis*), a slightly smaller, stiff, pyramidal tree with purple cones, takes over from the Momi Fir and is itself eased out at higher altitudes by the subalpine species Maries Fir (*Abies mariesii*), a small tree again, barely reaching 23 metres (75 feet) and differing from the others in its grooved, glossy green leaves, much crowded together on the twigs. It is one of the most important trees in the subalpine forests of Japan. Growing above all the others is Veitch's Fir (*Abies veitchii*), the smallest of the Japanese firs and perhaps the most beautiful. Its narrow, conical shape, together with the bright silver bands on the undersides of the upturned leaves make this tree a very popular ornamental. The purple cones and the purplish, resinous buds are distinctive characteristics.

The Korean Fir (*Abies koreana*) is another alpine species confined to the volcanic island of Quelpaert and the mountains in the south of the Korean peninsula. A small tree, never more than 15 metres (50 feet) tall, it forms almost pure forests above 900 metres (3000 feet). Its short, notched, dark-green leaves are set radially round the shoots. The tree is of little economic importance but its habit of producing bluish cones in profusion when only about 1 metre (3 feet) tall has made it a very popular garden tree in many parts of the world.

Of the Chinese firs, the Manchurian Fir (*Abies holophylla*) is closely related to the Momi Fir and differs from it in that the cones have no visible bracts and the leaves are not notched at the apex. Delavay's Fir (*Abies delavayi*) also has very near relations or varieties which confuse observers. The type tree comes from south-west China where it grows to 30 metres (100 feet) in height, with slightly ascending branches and bright-green leaves curled down along their margins, hiding the white bands beneath but accentuating the bright-green midrib.

The purple cones of the Korean Fir are borne on trees as small as 0·9 metre (3 feet) tall.

The varieties *A.d. forrestii*, *A.d. fabri*, and *A.d. faxonia* (shown as separate species by some authorities) differ in small respects; but all of them are ornamental trees.

Farges Fir (*Abies fargesii*), a large tree reaching 30 metres (100 feet), with long, notched leaves, comes from north-west Hupeh and is the most beautiful of the Chinese firs. The alpine species, the Flaky Fir (*Abies squamata*), found growing at 3600 to 4200 metres (12 000 to 14 000 feet) in northern Szechwan is perhaps the most curious; its orange-brown bark rolls up in large, thin, papery layers and remains hanging on the bole. The Min Fir (*Abies recurvata*) also has flaky bark, but in vertical rolls; its leaves in the centre of the shoots curve backwards. It is also from Szechwan where it is found growing in extensive forests on the mountains above the Min River.

GENUS *Cedrus* true cedars

A genus of four species of closely related, large, evergreen trees found in the Mediterranean area and in the Himalayas. They have needle-like leaves borne in dense whorls on short, spur-like shoots. Their oval cones stand upright like those of *Abies*, but disintegrate only after at least two years.

The most famous of the genus is the Cedar of Lebanon (*Cedrus libani*). Praised in the Psalms for its strength and size, this tree was the epitome of all that was good and majestic. Even so, this reverence did not save it from destruction. The fragrant, durable timber was in constant and overwhelming demand, not least by Solomon for his temple and

The Cedar of Lebanon grows huge branches from a short but massive bole.

Cedrus

61

Right
The blue variety of the Atlas Cedar is one of the most strikingly beautiful of all conifers.

Far right
Deodars growing in the Himalayan Kulu Valley. This cedar is one of India's most important timber trees.

many other projects for which he employed tens of thousands of slaves to fell the Cedars. No wonder the forests disappeared. There is now only a small remnant left in the Lebanon although the tree is still plentiful in the Taurus Mountains. Massive Cedars 30 metres (100 feet) tall and 7·5 metres (25 feet) in girth are among the most picturesque trees to be seen around the world, especially on lawns in big gardens where their huge, spreading branches arising from low down on the bole and higher up as the tree forks, support dense plates of dark-green foliage in layer after layer, ending in a flat, table-like top, and shading a huge area of ground. It is these level branches which distinguish the Lebanon Cedar from the Atlas Cedar (*Cedrus atlantica*), a native of those mountains in Algeria and Morocco, whose branches tend to grow out from the trunk in an ascending fashion, and never spread out over so wide an area. The leaves, too, have a slightly bluish tinge and the cultivar 'Glauca', with bright, blue-grey leaves, is one of the most attractive conifers we have for ornamental planting.

The Cyprus Cedar (*Cedrus brevifolia*) is very like the Lebanon species but is confined to that island. It has much shorter needles than its near relative and never has the flat top, nor does it reach great sizes.

The Deodar (*Cedrus deodara*) is the Himalayan species and the most elegant of the four. It is found at elevations up to 3000 metres (10 000 feet) in the west of mountains, from Kumaon north-west to Afghanistan where it grows to great sizes. Trees 55 metres (180 feet) tall and 3 metres (10 feet) in girth are not unusual. It differs from the other cedars in its gracefully drooping branches and its long, spire-like leading shoot, also drooping; and the leaves of young trees have a silvery tinge. The Deodar is an important timber tree in India, used extensively for building and railway sleepers, and outside its native country it is much planted as an ornamental.

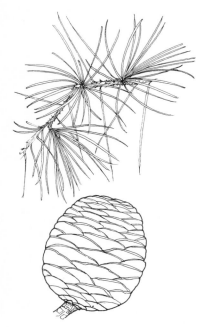

The whorls of needles and the oblong cone of the Deodar.

The bright, springtime green of a European Larch at Grisedale, Cumbria, England.

Larix

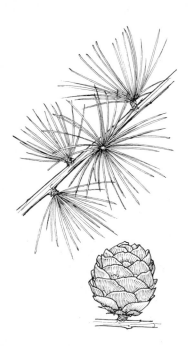

The whorls of deciduous leaves and the soft, upright cone of the European Larch.

GENUS *Larix* larches

A genus of ten species of large, deciduous trees spread widely across the Northern Hemisphere. The main leaves are borne in whorls on spurs like the cedars, and those on the terminal shoots are spirally arranged, singly along the stem. The cones are small, soft, and erect, remaining on the tree for some years after dropping their seed.

The European Larch (*Larix decidua*) is distributed naturally throughout the Alps of central Europe and northern Russia and is an important planted timber tree all over northern Europe. It reaches considerable sizes, especially in cultivation in lowland areas where it can top 45 metres (150 feet) and girth 4.5 metres (15 feet), and, being deciduous with a very light crown, it is often planted in mixture with hardwoods such as beech to protect them in the early stages. The beautiful light green of this fast-growing tree in spring, dotted with the bright red female flowers, and the russet hues in autumn give it a special place in forestry, because it not only adds variety to the landscape, it also produces a valuable timber used in large sizes for boat skins, telegraph poles, and railway sleepers, and in the smaller sizes for fencing, pit props, and many rural uses.

The Japanese Larch (*Larix kaempferi*) is a slightly smaller tree, rarely exceeding 30 metres (100 feet), but very similar in appearance to the European species. It differs in having reddish rather than straw-coloured twigs, and the cones are more squat with the edges of the scales turned down and outwards like the petals of a rose. It is endemic to the subalpine region of central Japan where it is an important timber tree as well as being a very popular ornamental. It is planted extensively outside its native country, especially in Britain where it has crossed with the European Larch to produce the Hybrid Larch (*Larix × eurolepis*), or Dunkeld Larch, after the Scottish estate on which the cross occurred in 1897. This tree grows with great vigour under cultivation and appears to be immune to some of the fungal diseases to which the European species is susceptible. In appearance it is very like its Japanese parent but the shoots are paler and the cone scales, although spread open a little, are not turned down at the tips.

The largest and most impressive member of the genus, and the most important American species, is the Western Larch (*Larix occidentalis*) whose natural range is restricted to the high valleys and mountain slopes of south-east British Columbia and the upper Columbia River Basin between the Rockies and the Cascades. Here it grows to great sizes, exceeding 60 metres (200 feet) in height and 4·5 metres (15 feet) in girth with a tall, straight trunk furnished with a slender, pyramidal crown of short, horizontal branches. It makes a magnificent tree; in mixture with pines and firs all of which it overtops with its satiny, pale-green foliage, the huge cinnamon-coloured bole rising through a layer of scarlet maples, it is an unforgettable autumn sight on the mountain slopes. Fine hairs on the young twigs and cones with long bracts extending as spines well beyond the scales, distinguish this tree from other larches. The timber is hard and fine grained, and one of the heaviest of all conifers and has many uses in construction work.

A much smaller tree is the Tamarack (*Larix laricina*) found from the Arctic Circle in Alaska and Canada, and eastwards right across that country to the Atlantic seaboard and south into New England, Minnesota, and Illinois. A straight and slender tree, seldom more than 18 metres (60 feet) tall, it consorts with poplars, birches, and willows and other hardy trees in a hostile climate and, like them, casts its leaves as the bitter winter approaches. The timber is very durable in contact with the soil and is used for telegraph poles, fencing, and for boat building.

The third American species is an alpine tree, Lyall's Larch (*Larix lyallii*), which has a very local distribution near the timber line at 1800 to 2100 metres (6000 to 7000 feet) on the Cascade Mountains. Again it is a small tree, some 15 metres (50 feet) tall, and is distinguished from its relatives by its pale, blue-green leaves which are quadrangular in cross-section. None of these American larches fares well in Europe.

The Siberian Larch (*Larix russica*) differs only in very small detail from the European species. It has more slender leaves and the cone is rounder, but its distribution as a high latitude rather than an alpine species draws the distinction. It is found mixed with other trees in north-east Russia and west Siberia where the winters are long and harsh and

Above
Unlike most conifers, larches shed their leaves in winter.

Left
The pink cones of the Japanese Larch show the typical reflexed scales like rose petals.

the summers short and hot with little or no transition period. The timber has many local uses.

The Sikkim Larch (*Larix griffithiana*) is a small but beautiful tree with long, pendulous branches and a spreading crown. It is found at high elevations of between 2700 and 3300 metres (9000 and 11 000 feet) in the Himalayas of Sikkim, Bhutan, and Tibet where it grows to about 15 metres (50 feet) together with pines at the lower levels and in pure stands over rhododendrons at the upper limits, preferring the rocky moraines in the steep, high valleys. The cylindrical cones of this species, standing 10 millimetres (4 inches) tall among the long, light-green leaves, are much bigger than those of other larches except the Chinese Larch (*Larix potaninii*), a very similar, graceful tree from south-west China, which has cones only slightly smaller.

Further east the Dahurian Larch (*Larix gmelinii*) stretches eastwards across Siberia to Manchuria and Korea and hybridizes with the Siberian species in the west of its range when it splits into a number of varieties on some of the small islands off the Pacific coast.

GENUS *Pseudolarix*
(*pseudo*, false, *larix*, larch)

A genus of one species of large, deciduous trees closely related to the larches but with cones which break up when ripe, wider, longer leaves and club-shaped spur shoots which lengthen annually with persistent scales. The cones, too, look different from those of the larches, their scales being triangular and sharp pointed.

The Golden Larch (*Pseudolarix amabilis*) is a native of eastern China where, in a restricted area in Chekiang and Kiangsi provinces, it grows to 36 metres (120 feet) tall, well furnished with symmetrical branches. Outside its native country this tree is usually seen as a small, flat-crowned specimen in big collections and gardens where its brilliant, golden-yellow colouring makes it a fine addition to the autumn scene.

GENUS *Picea* spruces
(the old Latin name for pitch pine)

A genus of some fifty species of large, evergreen trees distributed over the whole Northern Hemisphere, with the exception of Africa, and resembling the firs (*Abies*) in many respects but differing from them in having leaves that are usually sharper and stiffer but which, when they

The whorls of long, curved, deciduous leaves of the Golden Larch.

fall, always leave their short, peg-like stalks adhering to the twigs, making them rough to the touch. Their cones, too, differ, in that they are always pendulous when ripe and are usually borne at the tips of the branches. Many spruces are very important timber trees.

Towering over the seven North American species is the Sitka Spruce (*Picea sitchensis*) native to a narrow Pacific coastal strip, about 80 kilometres (50 miles) wide, running 3200 kilometres (2000 miles) from Kodiak Island in Alaska south to Mendocino County in north California. It ranks with the Redwood and the Douglas Fir as one of America's fastest-growing conifers. Heights of over 45 metres (150 feet) are quite usual with girths of 2·4 metres (8 feet) and more. The largest tree measured was 87 metres (286 feet) tall and over 4·8 metres (16 feet) in girth. These mature trees are extremely impressive with swollen, buttressed bases and towering, slightly tapering boles with flaking bark, supporting a conical crown of small branches bearing stiff, intensely prickly, blue-green needles with two white bands on the lower surface. The cones are very small for so large a tree. The pale-brown, soft wood, remarkably strong for its weight, has many specialist uses as well as for building timber. It was used for aeroplane construction during World War II, and piano sounding boards are made from it. The Sitka Spruce has become an important tree for afforestation in other countries, especially those with an oceanic climate such as Britain.

The stiff, spiky needles, typical spruce leaf scars, and small, pendulous cone of the Sitka Spruce.

In contrast to the huge, commercially important Sitka, the Brewer's Spruce (*Picea breweriana*) is a smaller, much rarer tree confined to a few isolated areas high in the Siskuyu and Shasta Mountains. It is remarkable for the multitude of fine, string-like branches hanging like curtains from the main limbs, which in young trees makes it one of the most elegantly beautiful of all conifers. Older trees may have branchy boles and only small crowns, but these are rarely seen, so inaccessible is their habitat, and the tree is chiefly noticeable for the number of fine, open-grown specimens which are to be found in gardens and arboreta in many countries throughout the world.

Another western North American spruce which is best known as an ornamental tree is the Blue Spruce (*Picea pungens*) which comes from the central Rocky Mountain region where, at elevations of 1800 to 2400 metres (6000 to 8000 feet), it grows some 36 metres (120 feet) tall, forming a dense, symmetrical pyramid of branches bearing dull grey-green to pale-blue stiff, sharp, four-angled needles. Its colour, which varies in intensity and shade according to the age of the tree and the site, distinguishes it from all except one other spruce. The cultivar 'Glauca' which is a bright, pale, powdery blue is much planted as an extremely attractive and effective ornamental.

Very like the Blue Spruce in many ways is Englemann Spruce (*Picea engelmannii*) whose blue-green crowns are a feature at 2400 to 3600 metres (8000 to 12 000 feet) in the high Rocky Mountains from Yukon to Arizona. The leaves are much softer than those of the Blue

The string-like branches hanging like curtains from the main limbs give the Brewer's Spruce a special elegance.

A Blue Spruce against a background of cypress hedges in the Chiltern Hills, Buckinghamshire, England.

Spruce and, in young trees, they are decidedly silvery, with an unpleasant smell when crushed. The shoots, too, are covered with fine hairs for the first three years, unlike those of the Blue Spruce. The tree is also an important source of timber but it is rarely obtainable in large dimensions. Although the tree is the largest of the high mountain species, it rarely exceeds 30 metres (100 feet) and even these sizes are difficult to extract from their mountainous domain.

The Black Spruce (*Picea mariana*) and the White Spruce (*Picea glauca*) share the same transcontinental range from Alaska to Newfoundland including the whole of Canada and into the Great Lakes and Pennsylvania. They also share many characteristics including a height growth averaging about 23 metres (75 feet). But the Black Spruce's cones are very much smaller, produced profusely in clusters along the branches, and round in shape; while those of the White Spruce are larger and cylindrical, and grow on the ends of twigs. The White Spruce, too, does have a slightly whitish tinge to its leaves, hence the name, while the Black Spruce is dark green. The timber of both species is virtually the same and marketed as such for pulp and general constructional purposes.

Above
The long, pendulous cone of the
Norway Spruce.

Right
The narrow, spire-like Serbian Spruce
has needles with a bluish tinge on
their undersides.

The natural range of the Red Spruce (*Picea rubens*) also coincides with the previous two in its northern limit of Nova Scotia and Quebec where it is found at sea-level but stretches south along the Appalachians into Georgia where it is seldom found below 1500 metres (5000 feet). The tree grows up to 24 metres (80 feet) tall in favourable situations and is distinguished from the other species by its crowded, incurved, grass-green needles and the long awl-shaped points on the outer bud scales. The shoots are covered with reddish hairs and the cones are red in colour, hence the name. Its light-coloured timber with long, straight fibres, makes it a favourite for pulping.

The most widespread European species is the Norway Spruce (*Picea abies*), a native of the mountain regions of central and northern Europe and on into western Russia. It is one of the most important forest and timber trees in Europe and is known in almost every household as the Christmas Tree. In some of the old natural stands in the Vosges and elsewhere, trees of 55 metres (180 feet) tall can still be seen, their tall, reddish, tapering stems and dense, dark-green crowns giving us a glimpse of the great forests of old. The tree does not grow naturally in Britain but has been planted there since before 1500 and is an important ingredient of many of the new forests. The timber is cream coloured, soft, straight grained, elastic, and light, giving it many uses.

The only other European member of this genus is the Serbian Spruce (*Picea omorika*) which has a very limited distribution on rocky limestone soil in the Drina Valley in Yugoslavia. It differs from the Norway Spruce in being remarkably slender and spire-like in habit, in having shorter, blunter, and bluish-green leaves with two white bands on the underside, and smaller cones. A hardy, graceful tree, strictly conical yet ornamental and, although it is usually seen in large gardens and parks, sometimes in close groups of three or four, it is also planted in smaller gardens because its narrow habit occupies relatively little space. Its tolerance of chalky soils is another factor in its favour.

The Oriental Spruce (*Picea orientalis*) comes from the Caucasus and southwards into Asia Minor, where it grows in high country between 600 and 2100 metres (2000 and 7000 feet) elevation, and is widespread in its distribution, often reaching 52 metres (170 feet) in height and 3·6 metres (12 feet) in girth. Old specimens, open grown, tend to be broadly columnar and young trees more conical, but the leaves distinguish this species. They are the shortest leaves of all the spruces and cling shiny green close to the shoots, looking like a lizard's tail. Attractive though the foliage is, the branching is often twisted and haphazard giving the tree, especially when young, an untidy look, less attractive to gardeners. The timber is much the same as the Norway species and takes its place in the eastern Mediterranean region.

The shiny green, short, clinging needles of the Oriental Spruce.

A Morinda Spruce at Yasmarg,
Kashmir showing the typical, hanging
shoots.

The Siberian Spruce (*Picea obovata*) is the most widespread of the genus stretching right across northern Europe, through Russia to Siberia, and on to Manchuria. Superficially it resembles the Norway Spruce, which it replaces in Europe wherever the climate is very severe, but it has more slender leaves more pressed down upon the shoots and a single leaf projecting from each side of the side buds. The cone, too, is about half the length of the Norway's. It is a tree of the taiga forming huge forests in the northern high latitudes.

Both the Indian spruces have beautiful pendulous branches. The Morinda Spruce (*Picea smithiana*) is a native of the western Himalayas from Afghanistan to Nepal and is found growing at between 2100 to 3600 metres (7000 and 12 000 feet) in mixed coniferous forest. Its long, incurved leaves, tapering to a sharp point, on hanging shoots, distinguish it from other spruces, even from Schrenk's Spruce (*Picea schrenkiana*), a central Asian species from Turkestan, which has much denser, shorter leaves. The Morinda Spruce reaches 60 metres (200 feet) in height producing large timber much used for many purposes in India. It is a fine ornamental in large gardens, particularly as a full-grown tree when the pendulous shoots are long and graceful.

The Sikkim Spruce (*Picea spinulosa*) comes from the east Himalayas, Sikkim, and Bhutan reaching similar sizes at the same elevations as the Morinda species, from which it differs in its shorter leaves which grow all round the pendulous shoot, pointing forward. They are grey-green above with two bluish bands beneath. Trees of up to 67 metres (220 feet) tall have been reported, making this the largest of the Asiatic species. It seems to be less hardy than the Morinda and is thus less frequently seen as an ornamental, though it is very quick growing in favourable conditions.

The Chinese Spruce (*Picea asperata*), a tree up to 30 metres (100 feet) tall in its native western China, is very similar to the Norway Spruce but the leaves are more rigid and are radially arranged on the shoot. The cone, too, is very much shorter. It has a number of varieties, some differing only minutely, and all very confusing. Also from western China is the Likiang Spruce (*Picea likiangensis*), a similarly variable tree with stiff, bluish, sharp needles and bearing a profusion of bright red, upright, male flowers in spring which look like lights on a Christmas tree. In its native Szechwan it grows 30 metres (100 feet) or more tall and is found up to 3600 metres (12 000 feet) elevation. It is sometimes seen in large gardens where its Maytime floral display is its chief attraction, although it is a shapely tree at all times.

The Japanese Tiger-tail Spruce (*Picea polita*) is the spruce of the cool, temperate regions of Honshu, Shikoku, and Kyushu where it is a medium-sized tree growing to 27 metres (90 feet) in height in scattered stands and in mixture with hardwoods. Its stout, stiff, sickle-shaped leaves with sharp points distinguish this species from the others and, radiating all round the shoot, give it its name. In Japan it is often planted as an ornamental and the timber is used for building and pulp.

The two subalpine species, Alcock's Spruce (*Picea bicolor*) and the Saghalin Spruce (*Picea glehnii*), are both large trees and are very similar to look at but the former has yellowish-green cones and the latter purplish brown. Both trees grow to over 30 metres (100 feet) tall, the former in central Japan and the latter in Hokkaido. The even-grained timber is used for building and packaging and, in the best grades, for musical instruments.

The Hondo Spruce (*Picea jezoensis*) is the most important tree in northern Japan and extends to the Kuriles as well as to Korea and Manchuria. The tallest of the Japanese spruce, it reaches 45 metres (150 feet) in height and the leaves are somewhat similar to those of the Sitka Spruce to which it has some natural affinity. The timber is extensively used for construction work, furniture, and pulping.

The red male flowers of the Likiang Spruce give a fine springtime display.

The drooping, elegant symmetry of the Western Hemlock.

The soft, widely spaced leaves and the small, round cone of the Western Hemlock.

GENUS *Tsuga* hemlocks
(the Japanese name for hemlock)

A genus of nine species of large, evergreen trees from North America, the Himalayas, and eastern Asia related to the spruces but with smaller, soft, delicate leaves and very small, rounded cones.

The Western Hemlock (*Tsuga heterophylla*) is the senior member of the genus. It is a magnificent, stately tree and a very important component of the great coniferous forests which lie on the Pacific coastal strip of north-west America. It is found from Prince William Sound in Alaska right down south to just north of San Francisco, reaching its greatest development in moist locations on the western slopes of the Cascades and in the rainforests of the Olympic Peninsula. Here, the tree grows to huge proportions, sometimes as tall as 75 metres (250 feet) and more than 6 metres (20 feet) in girth, occasionally in pure stands but more often with Sitka Spruce and Douglas Fir. In the deep shade of these forests, the ground is carpeted with Hemlock seedlings which need less light than their competitors to grow and develop. In time, this tree becomes dominant although after fires the Douglas Fir is the first to become established ensuring its own dominance for decades, if not centuries. Always with a drooping leading shoot and pendulous branches, the Hemlock with its dark-brown, fissured trunk is easily picked out from its companions. Close up, too, the short, blunt leaves set comb-like either side of the shoot, and the little oval cones are distinctive. Despite the sizes available, the timber is more popular for pulping than for other uses although it is used for internal building work where great strength is not required. The tree is a popular ornamental and, like the Sitka Spruce, is much planted in forest plantations in countries with oceanic climates where its shade-bearing attributes make it useful for underplanting beneath other tree crops.

The Mountain Hemlock (*Tsuga mertensiana*) has the same natural geographical distribution as the western species but grows at greater elevations, up to 2100 metres (7000 feet) in the Cascades, and also extends further south in California. They stand dense blue-green against the mountain skylines sometimes as much as 36 metres (120 feet) tall but usually much less and often distorted by wind and weather. Young trees can be especially blue because they flank the mountain highways backed by maples and the tall brown boles of their elders. The leaves are arranged radially round the shoot, unlike all other Hemlocks, and the cones are also exceptional, being long and thin like those of the spruce. The tree is a very popular ornamental in America.

Above
Old Mountain Hemlocks near Crater Lake, Oregon.

Left
The small cones of the Western Hemlock opening to release their seeds.

The Eastern Hemlock (*Tsuga canadensis*) is a native of the eastern United States and adjacent Canada, stretching from Maine to Minnesota and eastwards to Michigan. It is a small and less impressive tree than the western species. Nevertheless, a tree of 48 metres (160 feet) has been recorded but 18 to 24 metres (60 to 80 feet) is more usual. The Eastern Hemlock has a flatter crown than the western tree because of a tendency to fork, and the foliage differs from the western and all other hemlocks in having a row of leaves upside down along the length of the twig showing their white undersides. The cones are among the smallest of any conifers. Again, like the western species, this tree casts dense shade in pure stands beneath which only its own seedlings can survive. The timber is much the same as the western tree and is in increasing demand as other timbers become scarcer.

The Carolina Hemlock (*Tsuga caroliniana*) is a smaller tree again, and rare, found only in the Blue Ridge Mountains of the Alleghenies from Virginia, through North Carolina into Georgia, and growing usually singly along the rocky banks of streams. It is some 12 to 15 metres (40 to 50 feet) tall with many short, stout, pendulous branches and a pyramidal crown. The leaves are slightly longer than those of the eastern species and they stand out all round the twig. The timber is of little commercial importance but the tree is a sought-after ornamental in the United States, although neither it nor the eastern tree does so well in Europe as the western species.

The Himalayan Hemlock (*Tsuga dumosa*) occurs in those mountains from Kumaon eastwards to Bhutan at altitudes varying from 2400 to 3000 metres (8000 to 10 000 feet) growing in groups with Morinda Spruce, larch and rhododendrons. It is a beautiful tree sometimes as tall as 36 metres (120 feet) and frequently covered with ferns and lichens, which accentuate its weeping habit, making a very graceful pyramid. The leaves are the longest of all hemlocks and are grooved with two white bands beneath. The timber is too inaccessible for commercial use. Unfortunately, the tree does not fare well in Europe where it always breaks into multiple trunks spoiling its shape.

The Chinese Hemlock (*Tsuga chinensis*) is a tree of wide distribution in central and western China but is rarely seen elsewhere. Its foliage resembles the western American species but has pale-green bands beneath the leaves. In its native land it grows to 30 metres (100 feet) or more in height and the wood is used there for building purposes.

The Northern Japanese Hemlock (*Tsuga diversifolia*) is the most important tree in the subalpine coniferous forests of central and northern Honshu. It grows to heights of about 24 metres (80 feet) and is distinguished from its compatriot relative by its hairy shoots and its nearly stalkless cones. The Southern Japanese Hemlock (*Tsuga sieboldii*) is the dominant tree in the temperate coniferous forests in central and southern Honshu as well as in Shikoku and Kyushu. It has smooth shoots and cones with distinctly crooked stalks. Both species sometimes overlap in central Honshu and, very rarely, an intermediate form between them is found. The timber of both trees is much prized as building material.

GENUS *Pseudotsuga* Douglas firs
(*pseudo*, false, *tsuga*, hemlock)

A genus of five species of large, evergreen trees from North America, China, and Japan related to the firs (*Abies*). Their leaves are soft and do not leave a circular scar on the twig when they fall. The buds are sharp pointed like those of the beech and unlike other conifers, and the pendulous cones have three-pronged bracts projecting beyond the scales and pointing towards the tip.

The Douglas Fir (*Pseudotsuga menziesii*), one of the world's most important and valuable timber trees, grows extensively through western North America. From north of Vancouver Island down through Washington and Oregon to northern California, the typical or green variety is one of the chief components of the huge coniferous forests of the Pacific coastal strip. Inland the blue variety extends down the Cascade Mountains to the Sierra Nevada in northern California. It is the green Douglas which is the more valuable and forms the greatest and most impressive trees. In old stands, such as the Cathedral Grove on Vancouver Island, the great trees stand, with hardly room enough to walk between them, 82 metres (270 feet) or more

A stand of Douglas Firs with young trees growing beneath them.

Above
Douglas Fir cones showing the typical, three-pronged bracts.

Right
The orange-red bark of Scots Pines in the evening sunlight.

The soft needles, pointed buds, and the cone with three-pronged, projecting bracts of the Douglas Fir.

tall and nearly 12 metres (40 feet) in girth, on a mossy carpet amidst a mass of Sword Ferns. The great boles, clad in furrowed bark, are hung with lichens, and the volume of timber in each and in all of them collectively is breathtaking. Such virgin stands are rare but even in second growth areas, those where the old trees were felled a century ago to be replaced by their offspring, the charm of these lovely trees is still irresistible. The tallest Douglas Fir ever felled and measured was 117 metres (385 feet) tall and 9 metres (30 feet) in girth, making it taller in its time than the present-day record holder, the Redwood of 110 metres (367 feet). The timber is light red in colour, and very strong and durable. The immense size of the trees enables the cutting of timber free of knots and defects for constructional uses and the slicing of veneers for plywood of large dimensions. The Douglas Fir has become an important forest tree in Europe, particularly in Britain where it is also grown in parks and large gardens as an ornamental, and also in New Zealand.

The other American species, the Large-coned Douglas Fir (*Pseudotsuga macrocarpa*) is a much smaller tree, seldom more than 21 metres (70 feet) tall confined to rocky slopes on the mountains of southern California. Its leaves are widely spaced all round the shoot and pointing forward. The cones are the distinguishing feature, being the biggest of the genus, up to 178 millimetres (7 inches) long. The tree is of no economic importance.

The Japanese Douglas Fir (*Pseudotsuga japonica*) is a rare tree confined to the Kii Peninsula of Honshu and the eastern part of Shikoku where it receives a measure of protection and conservation. It grows to upwards of 30 metres (100 feet) in height and is distinguished from the other species by its hairless shoots and its small cones. It is very rare in cultivation outside Japan. The other two Asiatic species, the Chinese Douglas Fir (*Pseudotsuga sinensis*) and Wilson's Douglas Fir (*Pseudotsuga wilsoniana*) are also rare. The former comes from western China and the latter from south-west China and Taiwan. Both have cones with much shorter trident bracts than the other species, and both grow to 24 metres (80 feet) or so.

Pinus

The bluish-green, paired needles and the ovoid cone of the Scots Pine.

An old Austrian Pine beside a new road cut through indigenous forest in Yugoslavia.

GENUS *Pinus* pines

A genus of some eighty species of mostly large, evergreen trees from all regions of the Northern Hemisphere and in one case crossing the equator into Java. They differ from all other conifers in having long, needle-like foliage in bundles of two, three, or five emerging from a single sheath. The woody cones vary in shape from round to long and cylindrical and develop only in their second year, often remaining on the branches for years after dropping their seeds. In general, pines prefer dry sites and well-drained soils.

The best-known, two-needle pine in Europe is the Scots Pine (*Pinus sylvestris*) which has the widest distribution of the genus, stretching from Spain right across northern Europe, through Siberia to the Pacific coast. It differs from all other two-needle pines in having bluish green, often twisted, foliage, reddish bark on the upper trunk, and bigger branches. In old age, it is distinguished by its characteristic flat top and spreading crown. Rarely does it exceed 30 metres (100 feet) in height or 1·5 metres (5 feet) in girth but one tree, blown down in Scotland and found to have 331 annual rings, was 39 metres (128 feet) tall and had a girth of 4·8 metres (16 feet). Old, possibly virgin, stands of this beautiful tree, Britain's only native pine, can still be seen in Scotland, remnants of the old Caledonian Forest. In the evening light in August, with the purple heather beneath them, the bark of the pines seem almost afire

The characteristic umbrella shape of Stone Pines in Portugal.

with a reddish glow, taking us back thousands of years. The timber is excellent and is marketed under the name of 'redwood', and its uses are legion throughout Europe where it is the timber in everyday use.

The two-needled Corsican Pine (*Pinus nigra maritima*), and the Austrian Pine (*Pinus nigra nigra*), are very similar trees, the former with a limited distribution in Corsica, southern Italy, and Sicily but widely planted as a forest tree outside its range and the latter spread from the the Pyrenees to Asia Minor, with distinct if minor, geographical varities, but much less planted as a forest tree: more usually for shelter. The needles of these trees are longer and greener than the Scots Pine and the bark is a heavily ridged dark grey. They are large trees reaching 42 metres (140 feet) and, for pines, quick growing. The timber is coarser and weaker than the Scots Pine and much less in demand. Even so, the Corsican Pine's ability to grow on poor, dry, chalky soils and on coastal sites has made it ideal for pioneer afforestation. The rather coarse-leaved Austrian Pine is a valuable tree for windbreaks.

The Mountain Pine (*Pinus mugo*) is the smallest of the two-needle European pines, often only a bush high up in its native Pyrenees and Swiss Alps, but sometimes a small tree up to 12 metres (40 feet) tall at lower altitudes, and a sturdy, cone shape. The short, dense needles are grouped in whorls with a gap between each year's growth. The tree is of little economic importance but is useful for anti-avalanche planting at high elevations.

The Stone Pine (*Pinus pinea*) is found in the Mediterranean region from Portugal to Asia Minor where its broad, umbrella-shaped crown of shiny, dark-green, paired needles distinguish it from the other more pyramidal pines in the region. The large globular cones, too, are

The shiny, dark-green needles in bundles of five and the swollen, scaled cone of the Arolla Pine.

distinctive being some 150 millimetres (6 inches) long and weighing up to 340 grams (12 ounces). The seeds are edible, consumed under the names *pignons* and *pinocchi*. The timber has limited local uses.

The Maritime Pine (*Pinus pinaster*) occupies the same range as the Stone Pine westwards of Greece, and also extends into Algeria, but it looks quite different, having a much more open crown and purple instead of light-brown bark. The needles, too, are very long, up to 125 millimetres (5 inches), longer than any other two-needle pine. Being a tree of light, sandy soils and an important source of turpentine and resin, it is much planted both as a crop and for fixing windblown sand-dunes. In western France, particular in the Landes, there are extensive forests of this tree, and resin tapping is a considerable industry. In Portugal large areas of sand-dunes have been reclaimed by planting this tree.

Another two-needle species which is native to countries bordering the Mediterranean is the Aleppo Pine (*Pinus halepensis*), a smallish, domed tree up to 18 metres (60 feet) tall with slender, bright-green needles on grey branches, and very distinctive shiny, reddish cones. It is a tree which likes hot, dry areas and is very resistant to drought, being planted chiefly to prevent soil erosion and for resin tapping, particularly in Algeria.

The Bosnian Pine (*Pinus leucodermis*) is rare and of a very restricted distribution in the Balkan mountains, but it is worthy of mention because of its grey bark with white patches and its blue cones. It is extremely hardy, tolerates chalky soils, and, thus, is a very useful ornamental tree growing to some 18 metres (60 feet) in height.

There are no three-needle pines native to Europe, and there are only two five-needle species. The Arolla Pine (*Pinus cembra*) is found in the Alps and the Carpathians growing up to 21 metres (70 feet) tall at elevations of between 1500 and 2400 metres (5000 and 8000 feet). The tree is columnar in shape with short, horizontal branches densely covered with bluish-grey needles in bundles of five. The egg-shaped

An old Arolla Pine high in the Alps above Grindelwald, Switzerland.

Tapping a Maritime Pine for turpentine in Portugal.

cones are blue in the summer, becoming shiny, reddish-brown as the year proceeds. The lightweight, straight-grained wood is used for the indoor finish of houses and chalets and for local wood-carving industries. The other species is the Macedonian Pine (*Pinus peuce*) found in three small areas in Bulgaria and the western Balkan mountains. It much resembles the Arolla Pine in size and habit but the smooth green shoots are distinct.

The American two-needle pines are the least numerous of the three groups in that country. The Lodgepole Pine (*Pinus contorta*) is the most widespread species in north-west America growing from sea-level to some 3300 metres (11 000 feet) elevation from Alaska to California. The coastal region trees are sometimes as tall as 45 metres (150 feet) but up in the mountains they become progressively smaller and more gnarled, hence another name, the Screw Pine. Growing in dense stands, the young trees have tall, straight boles from which, in olden times, the Red Indians made their tepees or lodges. The short, yellow-green needles are untidily twisted on the often short and contorted branches. The timber works well and has many uses, and the tree has been planted in several countries, particularly Britain and New Zealand, where the mountain race has grown well on upland peats and other soils where drainage is impeded.

From coastal California comes the Bishop Pine (*Pinus muricata*), a tree reaching 24 metres (80 feet) in height and found growing on rocky headlands. It has long, dark-green needles and resinous buds, unlike other two-needle pines. The large, prickly cones remain on the tree for up to seventy years in annual groups spaced down the branches.

In the north-east of America the Red Pine (*Pinus resinosa*), is a two-needle species which grows from Nova Scotia to Pennsylvania and westwards to Manitoba and Minnesota. Widely known as the Norway Pine, after a village of that name in Maine, this tree reaches 24 metres (80 feet) or so in height, its clean, straight, red trunk being a familiar feature of eastern Canada and north-eastern United States. The dark-green, slender leaves snap cleanly when bent double, unlike those of any other pine. The timber is important commercially and has many constructional and other uses. The other two-needle pine with a wide distribution in the east of the country is the Short-leaf Pine (*Pinus echinata*), native from New York south to Florida and west into Texas,

The bright-green needles, in bundles of three, and the big asymmetrical cone of the Monterey Pine.

Missouri and Illinois. The tree is usually about 30 metres (100 feet) tall, and the short, slender, bluish-green needles distinguish it from other pines in this group. The cones' scales have deciduous spines, hence the specific name, from *echinus*, the Latin for a hedgehog. The timber being less resinous than most of its tribe, it is in great demand for a variety of constructional and other uses.

The Western Yellow Pine (*Pinus ponderosa*) is the largest of the three-needle pines and is one of the most widespread pines in America. It ranges from the Fraser River in British Columbia to Durango in Mexico, and from Nebraska to the Pacific Coast. It grows to an impressive size especially at elevations of between 1200 and 2400 metres (4000 and 8000 feet) on sites with a west and south aspect where summer rainfall is less than winter. Here trees of up to 60 metres (200 feet) tall and 7·5 metres (25 feet) in girth can be seen, their huge boles clad in great plates of orange-yellow bark, distinct from all other pines. The timber is widely used for general construction work of a light nature because, despite the large sizes available, it is not very strong. A very similar species is the Jeffrey Pine (*Pinus jeffreyi*) found in Oregon, the Coast Range of California, and the Sierra Nevada. It differs from the Yellow Pine in having needles which are bluish-green and cones which are much bigger and not at all prickly, and the bark is redder.

The Monterey Pine (*Pinus radiata*), like the Monterey Cypress, is confined to a very small area on the Californian coast, the largest stand being about 4000 hectares (10 000 acres) on and near the Monterey Peninsula. In these natural stands the tree rarely reaches more than 30 metres (100 feet) in height but again, like the Monterey Cypress, this pine grows remarkably well outside its native country. In New Zealand trees have reached 56 metres (185 feet) in eighty years and, in Australia, a forty year-old tree measured 47 metres (155 feet). This fast growth rate is the main reason for its success as a forest tree in many lands, particularly New Zealand where its capacity to form high-quality timber, when pruned and thinned, is unmatched by any other exotic. Open grown, these pines become very spreading with a domed crown and huge branches coming out from low down on the bole, which is covered with deeply fissured, grey bark. The bright-green needles distinguish the tree from all other three-needle pines and the cones which stay on the tree for thirty years or more, unlike those of the Bishop Pine, have no spines.

The massive bark plates on the bole of a Western Yellow Pine.

84

Above left
The beautiful bole of a Lace Bark
Pine, a Chinese species.

Above
The red buds and the long, bluish
needles of the Montezuma Pine.

forests in the Himalayas from Kashmir to Bhutan, is the most wide-spread and the chief resin producer in India. Exclusive to the north-west Himalayas and into Afghanistan is Gerard's Pine (*Pinus gerardiana*), a tree with pink-grey bark found at higher elevations where rainfall is scanty and snowfall heavy. To the east in the Assam Hills and north Burma is the Khasya Pine (*Pinus insularis*) which grows to 45 metres (150 feet) and has very fine, grass-like needles.

In China, is found the Lace Bark Pine (*Pinus bungeana*), a tree very similar to Gerard's Pine, but with even more attractive bark. It is smooth and greyish green in colour with small scales which peel off to leave areas of various colours from white to greyish purple. As an ornamental it is very effective, even if rare, with a broad, bushy crown and this very striking, quite un-pine-like bole.

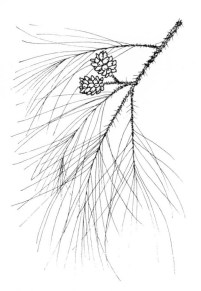

Above
Casuarinas bend to the tropical sea breezes.

Above right
Male cones and the long, wiry needles of the Bhutan Pine.

The switchy needles and cone-like fruits of the Swamp She Oak.

The Japanese White Pine (*Pinus parviflora*) is the five-needle pine of Japan where it grows extensively in mountain forests. It is a smaller tree than the other Japanese pines, rarely exceeding 21 metres (70 feet) in height, and its short, spreading, twisted, grey-green needles and the curious bun-shaped little cones erect on the branches distinguish it. The Korean Pine (*Pinus koraiensis*) also appears in Japan as a scattered subalpine tree in central Honshu, and very rarely, in Shikoku; but it is an important forest tree in Korea and Manchuria. It is very similar to the Arolla Pine but has longer leaves with whiter inner surfaces.

The Himalayan five-needle species is the Bhutan Pine (*Pinus wallichiana*), a beautiful and elegant tree which ranges all the way from Afghanistan to Bhutan at altitudes of 1800 to 3600 metres (6000 to 12 000 feet) and, next to the Deodar Cedar, is the most important timber tree in the Himalayas. Sometimes as tall as 48 metres (160 feet), with its grey bark and large, sweeping branches bearing long, leathery, bluish needles, it makes a fine sight in mixture with birch and firs in the high mountains.

The Chinese White Pine (*Pinus armandii*), found in western China, Korea, and Taiwan, is closely akin to the Himalayan species. It differs chiefly in the shape of the cone which is much stouter than that of the Indian tree; indeed, it is stouter than those of any five-needle pine and has wider scales. The Chinese tree is also sparser in the crown and altogether of smaller stature.

Family Casuarinaceae
GENUS *Casuarina* she oaks
(from *casuarinus*, a Cassowary, the twigs resembling the feathers of the bird)

A genus of some twenty-three, mostly Australian, evergreen trees with twigs modified into green, switchy needles, finely grooved along their length between whorls of minute, teeth-like leaves. The fruit is a round or oblong, cone-like structure.

The Swamp She Oak (*Casuarina equisitifolia*) is the best-known species outside Australia, growing wild in Malaysia and Indonesia, where it is a common sight in sandy coastal areas. Feathery and cypress-like in form and shape and up to 30 metres (100 feet) tall, these trees bend gracefully as the strong breezes off the tropical seas swish through their feathery fronds. They form most effective wind breaks, reaching 30 metres (100 feet) in twenty-five years and are also planted as ornamentals in parks and gardens. The wood, which is hard and red giving an alternative name, Beefwood, makes excellent firewood, a factor which has resulted in much devastation in natural stands. The Australian River Oak (*Casuarina cunninghamiana*) and Forest Oak (*Casuarina torulosa*) are both trees from subtropical parts of Queensland and the Northern Territories which grow to some 24 metres (80 feet) in height and are more important for ornamental planting than for their hard, reddish timber.

The Broadleaves

Family Salicaceae willows and poplars
(the Latin name for willow)
GENUS *Populus*

A genus of about thirty species of very fast-growing, mainly large, deciduous trees with resinous buds and flowers in catkins on separate male and female trees. They all come from northern temperate regions.

The White Poplar (*Populus alba*), indigenous to central and southern Europe and on into central Asia, is a tree which can reach 18 metres (60 feet) in height. It has furrowed, black bark on the bole which becomes grey or even yellowish white higher up and on the numerous stout branches. The bark is also pitted with black, diamond-shaped marks. The leaves are lobed, almost maple-like and covered with dense white hairs on their undersides and thinly spread on the upper surface. Easily mistaken for the White Poplar is the Grey Poplar (*Populus canescens*) although it is usually taller with a rounder crown and in every way bigger, with leaves which are rounder and a duller white beneath, and smooth on the upper surface. Neither tree is native to Britain but both have become naturalized there over the centuries.

The Aspen (*Populus tremula*), a native of Europe (including Britain), Asia Minor, and the Caucasus, is a lightly branched tree some 18 metres (60 feet) tall with ridged, brown bark at the base of the bole but mostly smooth and greenish on the rest of the tree, marked horizontally with **lenticels**, or breathing pores. The leaves are round with blunt teeth and characteristically flattened stalks which result in their constant trembling movement in even the slightest breeze. They turn bright yellow in the autumn. The timber is much in demand by the pulping industry.

The Black Poplar (*Populus nigra*) comes from northern and western Europe and is a big, spreading tree with huge lower branches arching out into a wide crown often 30 metres (100 feet) in height. The leaves are heart shaped, bright, glossy green above and pale green beneath, turning a soft yellow in the autumn. But it is the cultivar 'Italica', usually called the Lombardy Poplar because of its Italian origin, which is the best known of this species if not of the whole genus. Planted throughout the temperate world as screens, avenues, and as individual ornamentals, this tree is, to most people, the epitome of the word poplar. It is sometimes up to 30 metres (100 feet) tall and usually looks even taller; with its elegant, spire-like form, it deserves its widespread popularity.

Of the American poplars, the Black Cottonwood (*Populus trichocarpa*) reaches the greatest size. It comes from the Pacific north-west, ranging from southern Alaska to southern California. Its maximum development is reached in the Puget Sound area of Washington where trees of up to 60 metres (200 feet) were once reported. The leaves are thick and leathery, and the bark is grey and deeply furrowed. The logs, often very large from the older trees, give big timber used for barrels and boxes. The Eastern Cottonwood (*Populus deltoides*) is a common tree from Quebec to Florida and is generally smaller than the western species although heights of 45 metres (150 feet) have been reported from some southern areas. The leaves are large and D-shaped and between 100 and 180 millimetres (4 and 7 inches) long. The tree is remarkable for its rapid growth – heights of 30 metres (100 feet) in fifteen years have been recorded. Numerous hybrids between this tree and the European Black Poplar have arisen under the general name of *Populus* x *euramericana*,

Populus

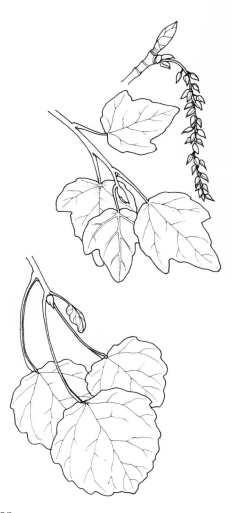

Top
The lobed, maple-like leaves and a female catkin of the White Poplar.
Bottom
The round, flat-stalked leaves of the Aspen.

Far left top
The silver backs of the White Poplar leaves shimmer in the summer sun.

Far left bottom
An isolated Eastern Cottonwood growing on the Montana prairies.

Left
Lombardy Poplars are most impressive when planted in lines or avenues.

Below
The flattened, slender stems of the Aspen leaves allow them to flutter in the slightest breeze.

Bottom
The Aspen catkins appear in early spring before the leaves.

and these are the trees, even quicker growing than the Eastern Cottonwood, which are planted throughout temperate countries for matches, wood wool, pulp, boxes, and crates.

The Balsam Poplar (*Populus tacamahaca*) ranges right across northern America from Alaska to Labrador, and in north-west Canada, where it reaches its greatest development, it is the biggest tree species, reaching 30 metres (100 feet) in height. The leaves are egg shaped and up to 150 millimetres (6 inches) long. The terminal buds on the twigs are 25 millimetres (1 inch) long, reddish brown, sharply pointed and coated with sticky, fragrant balsam, used in the drug trade. This tree, too, has produced a hybrid, with the Black Cottonwood – the unromantically named 'TT32' which is an extremely vigorous-growing, narrow tree, often planted for quick effect.

The American Quaking Aspen (*Populus tremuloides*), which has the widest distribution of all North American trees, thrives at all levels up to 3000 metres (10 000 feet) over the whole of north America from Alaska to Newfoundland and south along the Rockies to lower California. It is a very similar tree to the European Aspen but the leaves are more pointed and the bark is white like a birch, especially in young trees.

Of the Asiatic species, the Japanese Poplar (*Populus maximowiczii*), also found in Korea, Manchuria and north-west China, is a large tree up to 30 metres (100 feet) tall with shiny brown, resinous winter buds. The leaves are dark shiny green above and bluish green beneath with a net-like veination on both surfaces, and finely toothed margins. The wood is used for matches, packing cases, and pulp. In Japan, the tree is also planted along roadsides and in shelter belts.

The Chinese Necklace Poplar (*Populus lasiocarpa*), a native of central China, is one of the most remarkable poplars in cultivation. A tree up to 18 metres (60 feet) tall, its leaves are enormous, up to 380 millimetres (15 inches) long and 230 millimetres (9 inches) wide with a red midrib and stalk, the latter itself some 200 millimetres (8 inches) long. The catkins, too, are very long, nearly 250 millimetres (10 inches), the female ones carrying twenty or more small green fruits.

GENUS *Salix* willows

A genus of some 300 large and small deciduous trees, shrubs, and bushes from all north temperate areas, the arctic and south temperate zones, excluding Australia. The flowers, in catkins on separate male and female trees, open before the leaves.

The European White Willow (*Salix alba*) is found throughout that continent, in North Africa and central Asia usually along riversides in lowland valleys. It grows 24 metres (80 feet) in height on a trunk with dark-grey, thickly ridged bark and ascending branches pendulous at the tips. The buds are very small and pinkish, and the leaves are narrow, pointed, bluish green with white silky down that is dense on the underside and sparse above. A handsome tree, it yields a useful, soft timber but not as valuable as that from one of its cultivars 'Coerulea', the Cricket Bat Willow, which grows along the banks of dykes and streams and is distinguished from the white species by its slender purple shoots and its leaves which lose their down and are blue-grey beneath. They grow remarkably quickly, reaching 18 metres (60 feet) and producing the required size of butt for bat making in fifteen years.

Another cultivar 'Tristis', the Weeping Willow, is one of the most well loved of all willows. Growing beside lakes and ponds in parks and gardens, as well as on dry soils in suburbia, with long, slender, yellow shoots sweeping down to the water's surface, it is the first of all trees to become flecked with spring green as the leaves unfold, and many a small, unsuspecting front lawn has become immersed beneath its quickly enveloping shroud.

The Crack Willow (*Salix fragilis*) is a tree much like the White Willow when left to nature and has very much the same range, but it is usually seen pollarded and in England it is commoner than the White Willow in this state, growing beside most lowland rivers. Apart from the longer, bright-green leaves and the more open crown (when not pollarded) the curious way in which the twigs snap cleanly off the branches when smartly tapped near the base is a sure distinguishing feature.

Salix

Pollarded Crack Willows are a typical riverside feature in much of lowland Europe, particularly in southern Britain.

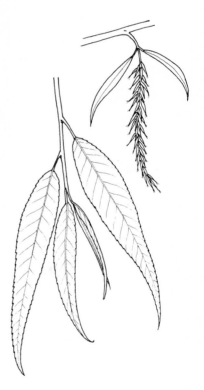

The narrow, pointed leaves and female catkin of the Crack Willow.

Left
The Weeping Willow is one of the first trees to show green in the spring and is especially attractive when growing near water.

Below
Cricket Bat Willows grow very quickly when planted along slow-flowing streams, becoming 18 metres (60 feet) tall in fifteen years.

The Goat Willow or Pussy Willow (*Salix caprea*) only occasionally grows as a tree and is more often a bush, but it is well known for the furry buds on the male trees which are curiously connected with Palm Sunday. These buds shine silvery on the tree for weeks before the golden stamens emerge to attract the early spring bumble bees. The tree is a native of Europe and north-west Asia and when open-grown on a good site can be as tall as 12 metres (40 feet). The oval, grey-green leaves have red stalks. Another species, inclined to be shrubby in the wild state, is the Bay Willow (*Salix pentandra*), which is found all over Europe from Norway to the Pyrenees and in Asia Minor. When planted in gardens, it grows up to about 15 metres (50 feet) and is one of the handsomest of willows, with its big glossy leaves and yellow midribs.

The largest of the American species is the Black Willow (*Salix nigra*) which grows along rivers and streams and on low-lying land throughout eastern Canada and United States. Trees of up to 42 metres (140 feet) tall with 12 metres (40 feet) of clear bole are found in the lower Mississippi Valley where they reach maximum development. The bark is very dark brown, or even black, and the long, narrow leaves are bright green. Unusual for a willow, the flowers appear at the same time, or sometimes after, the leaves. The timber is used for boxes,

Above
The 'pussy' buds of the Goat Willow are a well-loved and welcome sight in early spring.

Right
The Contorted Willow shows its strangely twisted branches in winter-time.

The winged fruits of the Caucasian Wing-nut are carried on long, hanging catkins.

crates, and charcoal. The Almond Willow (*Salix amygdaloides*) is a smaller tree reaching 21 metres (70 feet) in height, with the same range as the black species but differing from it in having broader leaves which are bluish green on their undersides.

A common willow in northern Japan and north-west China is *Salix sachalinensis*, a tree which grows some 15 metres (50 feet) tall along rivers and streams. It has long, deep-green, shiny leaves which are used as a substitute for tea in remoter parts, and ascending catkins. The other common Japanese willow is *Salix urbaniana*, a taller tree, reaching 24 metres (80 feet) in Hokkaido and Honshu. It has bigger, broader leaves which are bluish with net-like veins beneath, and pendant catkins. A much rarer tree in Japan, *Salix matsudana*, has produced a cultivar, 'Tortuosa', the Contorted Willow, which is often seen in gardens with its grossly distorted branches twisting and curling in all directions.

Family Juglandaceae
GENUS *Pterocarya* wing-nuts
(from *Pteron*, wing, *karyon*, nut)

A genus of eight species of deciduous trees from China, Japan, and the Caucasus with large, compound leaves, fruits in the form of small, winged nuts strung on long, hanging catkins, and pithy young twigs. The male and female flowers are on the same tree.

The Caucasian Wing-nut (*Pterocarya fraxinifolia*) is from the mountains of its name and eastwards into Persia, where on moist ground it is a large tree up to 30 metres (100 feet) tall, often branching low and forming a spreading crown. The leaves are some 460 millimetres (18 inches) long with between seven and twenty-seven opposite, stalkless, oblong leaflets. The nuts are about 19 millimetres ($\frac{3}{4}$ inch) in diameter including the circular wing which surrounds each one.

The Japanese Wing-nut (*Pterocarya rhoifolia*), a tree of up to 22·5 metres (75 feet) tall, is common along mountain streams in the cool, temperate regions of that country. The 300-millimetre (12-inch) long leaves have from ten to twenty leaflets, and the nuts have two separate lateral wings. The wood is used for making matches and sandals. The Chinese Wing-nut (*Pteryocarya stenoptera*) is very similar to the Japanese species but the leaf stalk between the leaflets has small wings or flanges on each side.

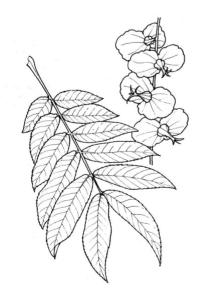

The large, ash-like compound leaf and the winged nuts on a hanging catkin of the Caucasian Wing-nut.

GENUS *Juglans* walnuts
(from *Jovis*, Jupiter and *glans*, a nut)

A genus of fifteen large, deciduous, nut-bearing trees from America and Asia, differing from the hickories by the pith in the young shoots being in thin, transverse plates which divide the hollow part into chambers, instead of being continuous. The male catkins are unbranched.

The Common Walnut (*Juglans regia*) is found from south-east Europe right across Asia to China, and is a large, spreading tree up to 30 metres (100 feet) tall with pale-grey bark, smooth between deep fissures on the bole and smooth on the upper stem and branches. The leaves are up to 300 millimetres (12 inches) long with seven to nine leaflets, the terminal one the largest and 150 millimetres (6 inches) long. The female flowers at the ends of the new shoots produce the round, smooth, dark-green fruits which contain the familiar walnut. The dark wood is superbly figured and much in demand for furniture, panelling, gunstocks, and many other uses.

The American Black Walnut (*Juglans nigra*) ranges throughout the western half of the United States and south-east Canada, but attains its best development on the alluvial soils of Maryland, Pennsylvania, and Virginia where trees of 45 metres (150 feet) in height are found, often with clean boles clad in black, ridged bark clear of branches for 18 metres (60 feet). The leaves have eleven to twenty-three leaflets and the round, green fruits, usually in pairs, contain a nut darker in colour and much less palatable than that of the common species, and the timber, although not so fine grained, is America's foremost cabinet wood, soft, brown, and finely marked. The Butter Nut (*Juglans cinerea*), with a very similar range as the black species, is a smaller, short-trunked, spreading tree, rarely more than 18 metres (60 feet) tall, but the leaves are much bigger at 500 millimetres (20 inches) long with fifteen to nineteen leaflets, and the pear-shaped fruits, three to five in a bunch and covered with sticky hairs, contain an oblong nut with a sweet, oily kernel, pleasant to eat fresh or pickled, hence the name. The tree is more valuable for its nuts and the shade it casts than for its timber.

Left
The pithy, green Walnut fruits eventually split to reveal the familiar walnuts.

Right
When mature, the Common Walnut has a huge, spreading crown giving shade over a wide area.

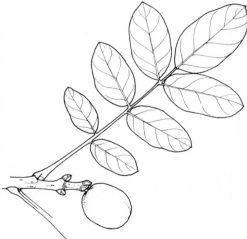

The compound leaf and fruit of the Common Walnut.

The Japanese Walnut (*Juglans ailantifolia*) is common throughout Japan along streams and in wettish places where it can reach 21 metres (70 feet) in height. The leaves are enormous, 0·6 to 0·9 metre (2 or 3 feet) long with eleven to seventeen leaflets, more abruptly tapered and blunter than other walnuts. The fruits, six to seven in a bundle are covered with sticky hairs and contain the walnuts which are sharply pointed at the top. The bark and the fruit pulp are used for dye making and poisoning fishes. The timber is used for furniture, gunstocks, and for wood carving. The closely related Manchurian Walnut (*Juglans mandshurica*) has slightly smaller, but still formidable, leaves and more pointed leaflets.

GENUS *Carya* hickories

A genus of twenty species of large- to medium-sized, deciduous trees from North America and China which differ from the walnuts in having solid pith in the shoots and the male flowers on a three-pronged catkin.

The largest of the genus is the Pecan (*Carya pecan*), an important tree not for its timber but because of its edible nuts. The tree's natural range is from Iowa south to Texas and Mexico, reaching its maximum size of some 51 metres (170 feet) in the Ohio basin. The leaves measure

A Pecan, 39 metres (130 feet) tall, planted by George Washington at Mount Vernon.

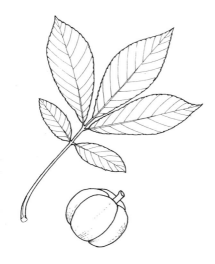

The five-leaflet (sometimes seven) compound leaf and four-lobed fruit of the Shagbark Hickory.

The bole of the Shagbark Hickory is covered in thin, rough plates of bark which peel vertically from both ends.

500 millimetres (20 inches) in length and have nine to fifteen short-stalked, finely pointed leaflets. The dark-brown nuts are borne on the ends of the branches in thin husks which break into four sections to release them. These empty husks often remain on the tree throughout the winter. The Pecan is cultivated in plantations, and several varieties have been developed which produce bigger nuts than the natural tree.

The Bitternut (*Carya cordiformis*) is a smaller tree than the Pecan which ranges further east and north into Canada, and rarely attains more than 30 metres (100 feet). Its most striking characteristic is the bright-yellow winter buds. The nine leaflets on the 230-millimetre (9-inch) long leaves are stalkless with uneven bases, and are yellow-green in colour. The round nuts, contained in thin, scaly husks in clusters of three are bitter and inedible. The timber is used for articles which require strength with elasticity, such as tool handles and, formerly, cart shafts and wheel spokes. It is also considered the best wood for smoking hams and bacon.

The Pignut (*Carya glabra*), found growing on dry ridges and in open fields from Vermont to Georgia to heights of 36 metres (120 feet), has relatively small leaves with five or seven yellow-green leaflets and nuts much resembling the Bitternut, although they are more pear shaped and not so bitter, even insipid. The Mockernut (*Carya tomentosa*), however, the most abundant of the southern hickories, has very fragrant leaves, up to 390 millimetres (15 inches) long, and nuts which have thick shells and a small amount of sweet kernel which is difficult to extract.

Two other hickories, the Shagbark Hickory (*Carya ovata*) and the Shell-bark Hickory (*Carya laciniosa*), both have shaggy bark, but that of the former is in strips which are sharply curved away from the bole at both ends, whereas the latter's are less obviously curved. Apart from the more restricted range of the Shell-bark, it has the largest leaf of all the genus, 740 millimetres (29 inches) long with five to nine (usually seven) leaflets, against the Shagbark's 690 millimetres (25 inches) with the same number but more pointed leaflets. All these hickories produce a valuable, strong, shockproof timber used in the sports' industry. The wood makes excellent firewood.

Betula

Above
The Chinese Red-barked Birch sheds its bark from the upper trunk and branches in thin, papery strips.

Above right
The white bark of the Silver Birch and its graceful, pendulous branches have rightfully earned it the name 'Lady of the Woods'.

Far right
A group of Himalayan Birches, somewhat disfigured by a snow-break, at 2900 metres (9500 feet) in the Kashmir Himalayas.

Family Betulaceae
GENUS *Betula* birches
(Latin name for birch)

A genus of forty species of comparatively short-lived, deciduous trees and shrubs with male and female catkins on the same tree. The male catkins are formed in the autumn, expanding in the spring. The bark is thin and papery, and frequently white. Birches grow on poor, light soils and the forest edge, in Europe, North America, the Himalayas, China, and Japan.

The Silver Birch (*Betula pendula*) is native throughout Europe and Asia Minor, and it is a tree of outstanding beauty and elegance, sometimes as much as 27 metres (90 feet) tall. In young trees the bark is shiny, reddish brown, later becoming white dotted with big, black diamonds, but the base of the bole is often black, rough, and fissured. The long, pendulous branches, purplish brown in winter and hung with bright-green, rounded, triangular leaves in summer, together with the white bole, make this tree a constant delight. Its very near relative, the Downy Birch (*Betula pubescens*) has an even whiter trunk but lacks the hanging branches. The shoots are covered with shiny white hairs and the leaves are rounder than the Silver Birch. These two birches have the same natural range, with the downy species tending to favour the damper ground. The timber of these birches is widely used for turnery, plywood, and pulp. A cultivar of the silver birch, 'Dalecarlica' has attractive, deeply cut leaves and a bole which becomes white at an early age.

The largest of the American species is the Yellow Birch (*Betula lutea*) which ranges from Newfoundland through to the Great Lakes and southwards along the mountains to Georgia. Trees 30 metres (100 feet) tall occur on good sites but 21 metres (70 feet) is more usual, with the oval crown covered in winter with the chestnut-brown, dormant male catkins, and in the summer with dark-green leaves with double-toothed margins interspersed with green, cone-like fruits. The bark on the upper trunk and limbs is silvery yellow, and on the lower trunk dark grey. A very similar tree, the Cherry Birch (*Betula lenta*), has a more restricted range from Maine through New York and down the Appalachians to Georgia. It differs from the yellow species in having darker, browner bark resembling that of the Cherry. The timber of both trees has the same uses as the European species, but the Cherry Birch wood is used also for distillation of birch oil and the sap makes birch beer.

The River Birch (*Betula nigra*) is between 18 and 24 metres (60 and 80 feet) tall, and is a tree of low-lying ground near lakes and rivers throughout the eastern half of the United States from New Hampshire to Florida and from Minnesota to Texas. Its cinnamon-coloured bark often hanging in tatters from the limbs and upper trunk, changing to dark brown, thick and scaly on the lower bole, distinguishes this tree. Especially so from the Paper-bark Birch (*Betula papyrifera*) which has bark of an almost pure whiteness right up into the smaller branches of the crown and all over the trunk, even in quite old trees. It is found from Labrador to Minnesota and south to the Great Lakes and New Jersey where it grows to some 24 metres (80 feet) in height. The bark was once used for making canoes and the timber is used for turnery, pulp, and fuel.

Now considered to be separate species, the Himalayan Birch (*Betula utilis*) and the White-barked Himalayan Birch (*Betula jacquemontii*) range across the Himalayas between the Kuram Valley and Bhutan where they grow up to 24 metres (80 feet) tall mixed with rhododendrons, firs, and maples at between 2100 and 4200 metres (7000 and 14 000 feet); at the high altitudes they are often gnarled and disfigured by snow. The Himalayan species has smooth, brownish-red bark, darker and thickened at the base of older trees, and in the White-barked the bark is white, peeling off in transverse strips. The leaves differ, too, those of the White-barked species having much more pronounced teeth around their margins. The wood and bark are used locally for building. Also closely related is the Chinese Red-barked Birch (*Betula albosinensis*) from central and western China where it can reach 30 metres (100 feet) tall, has bright, orange-red, peeling bark and comparatively large pointed leaves with toothed margins.

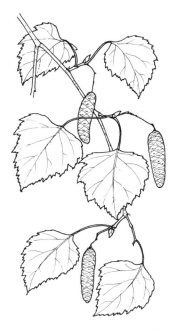

The rounded, triangular leaves with unevenly toothed margins, and female catkins of the Silver Birch.

In spring, the Common Alder's catkins give the crown an orange-yellow tinge.

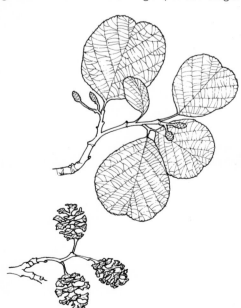

The shiny, dark-green leaves of the Common Alder with immature female catkins and opened, cone-like, black female catkins after casting their seeds.

The Japanese Red Birch (*Betula maximowicziana*), endemic to the central and northern parts of the country, grows up to 24 metres (80 feet) tall and is remarkable for the size of its leaves, 180 by 130 millimetres (7 by 5 inches), heart shaped, and more like those of a lime than a birch. These, together with the 130-millimetre (5-inch) long male catkins distinguish the tree from all other birches. The wood is used for furniture, plywood, and pulp. The Japanese Cherry Birch (*Betula grossa*), from central and southern areas, is very much like the American Cherry Birch except that the leaf margins are more heavily toothed; and the Japanese White Birch (*Betula mandschurica*) is almost indistinguishable from the European Silver Birch. To add to the confusion, Erman's Birch (*Betula ermanii*), from Japan and north-east Asia, is hard to separate from the Himalayan Birch except that the bark tends to hang in shreds from the branches in the crown.

GENUS *Alnus* alders
(Latin name for alder tree)

A genus of some thirty medium-sized, deciduous trees closely allied to the birches and ranging across the Northern Hemisphere, and into South America. They are mainly trees of moist sites and cool climates. The female catkins develop into woody, cone-like structures which remain on the trees after shedding the seed.

The Common Alder (*Alnus glutinosa*) is a native of Europe, western Asia, and North Africa where it is found beside lakes, ponds, rivers and streams from sea-level up to 450 metres (1500 feet). Growing up to 21 metres (70 feet) tall with a pyramidal crown of shiny, dark-green leaves, and a bole clad in dark, oak-like bark, this tree with the Willow is the typical waterside species throughout much of Europe, and easily distinguished from the willows by its dark, broad leaves and when leafless by the little black 'cones' which stay on the tree all winter. The timber, which is orange when first cut, was used for clog making. The Italian Alder (*Alnus cordata*) from southern Italy and Corsica, is a similar-sized tree but is more strikingly conic, and has very distinctive, heart-shaped leaves. The 'cones' are large, erect, and egg shaped. The tree is very quick growing [16·5 metres (55 feet) in twenty years] and thrives on much drier sites than the common species. The Grey Alder (*Alnus incana*), native to Europe and east into the Caucasus, is a hardy tree of wet, cold places with leaves which are grey on the undersides. A feature of all these alders is that their leaves stay green until they fall, never colouring like other species.

The cone-like, black, female catkins of the Common Alder persist on the tree throughout the winter.

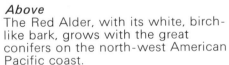

The largest American species is the Red Alder (*Alnus rubra*) which is confined to the Pacific coast region from Alaska to southern California where it consorts with the great in the coniferous forests of that region. It is easily mistaken for a birch because of its mottled-white bark, but the large, 150-millimetre (6-inch) long, yellow-green leaves and the brown 'cones' mark it as an alder. On good sites on the Olympic Peninsula, the tree grows to 39 metres (130 feet) tall and is the most valuable and plentiful of the few hardwoods of the Pacific coast. The pale-yellow wood is used extensively for furniture making. The White Alder (*Alnus rhombifolia*) is a smaller tree with a similar range and rounder leaves which are dark green above and light yellow-green and downy beneath. The only alder from the east of North America to reach any size, and this only occasionally, is the Seaside Alder (*Alnus maritima*) which can grow to 11·5 metres (35 feet) or so in damp riverine sites in Delaware and Maryland. Its lustrous green leaves, narrower at the base than at the tip, and its habit of flowering in the autumn distinguish this species, which is cultivated as an ornamental in some eastern United States.

The Himalayan Alder (*Alnus nitida*) is a large tree, upwards of 30 metres (100 feet) tall, which ranges from Kashmir to Kumaon at elevations of between 600 and 1200 metres (2000 and 4000 feet), fringing the banks of rivers and sometimes descending with them to the plains. The leaves are narrow, for an alder, wedge shaped at the base, and are usually coarsely toothed on the margins. Like the American Seaside

The bole of the European Hornbeam is often fluted and oval in section.

Alder, this tree flowers in the autumn. A rather smaller tree, the Nepalese Alder (*Alnus nepalensis*) occupies the eastern half of the Himalayas and on into China. This tree has similar leaves to the western species, but the 'cones' are borne crowded together, as many as twelve at a time, on a short panicle. It also flowers in the autumn.

The Japanese *Alnus hirsuta*, also found in Manchuria, grows up to 19·5 metres (65 feet) tall with nearly round, heavily toothed leaves, and with reddish hairs on the undersides. It is much planted for erosion control. Three other Japanese alders, all scarcely more than bushes, *Alnus firma*, *Alnus sieboldiana*, and *Alnus pendula*, have much narrower, more pointed leaves and are distinguished by their geographical distribution in the islands. They are all planted for erosion control.

GENUS *Carpinus* hornbeams
(Latin name for hornbeam tree)

A genus of twenty-six large, deciduous trees from north temperate regions, which have the male catkins enclosed in a bud during the winter, and the fruits in bunches, each with a wing attached. They are hardy and handsome trees, usually with smooth bark.

The European Hornbeam (*Carpinus betulus*) is found throughout Europe south of Sweden and west of the Pyrenees, and east into Asia Minor, usually growing up to 30 metres (100 feet) in company with Beech. It is a tree with a rounded crown of oval leaves with double-toothed

The oval, tooth-margined leaves and three-lobed, winged nuts of the European Hornbeam.

109

margins, very dark green above and yellowish beneath. The bole is smooth silvery grey and, in old trees, deeply fluted and often oval in section. The fruits are in clusters of about eight pairs of nutlets, each pair attached to the base of a green, three-lobed bract or wing. The timber is hard and bone-like, once used for the cogs and gears of water mills and currently for striking hammers in pianos. It is an excellent firewood and in the past the tree was much coppiced for fuel and for charcoal making. It also makes good hedges, tolerating regular shearing and retaining its dead leaves all winter. The cultivar 'Fastigiata' shaped like a brandy glass, with brighter green leaves, makes a very attractive street tree.

The American Hornbeam (*Carpinus caroliniana*) is a much less impressive tree, small and bushy and seldom more than 12 metres (40 feet) tall. It ranges over the whole of North America east of a line from Minnesota to Texas. Apart from being smaller than the European species, it has egg-shaped instead of pointed buds, and the leaves turn a reddish colour in the autumn rather than yellow. The timber is too small for commercial use.

Another much smaller species, the Eastern Hornbeam (*Carpinus orientalis*), is also native to Europe and Asia Minor. It has much smaller leaves and the seed wings are not lobed but entire like a small leaf.

The Japanese Hornbeam (*Carpinus japonica*) is a small tree some 15 metres (50 feet) tall and one of the commonest in the cool temperate region of the country. The leaves are narrow and pointed and up to 100 millimetres (4 inches) long. The wings on the nutlets are incurved forming a neat, cylindrical bunch. A closely related species, also with incurved seed wings, is *Carpinus cordata*, native to Japan and north-east China. Two other species, *Carpinus laxiflora*, confined to Japan and much used for fuel, and *Carpinus tschonoskii*, which extends to Korea and central China, are closely related to the European and American species.

GENUS *Ostrya* hop-hornbeams
(from Greek *ostrys*, hop-hornbeam)

A genus of seven species of medium-sized, deciduous trees from North America, Europe, Asia Minor, China, and Japan. They closely resemble the hornbeams but the male catkins are not enclosed in a bud and remain naked all winter. The nuts are enclosed in a bladder-like container on a hop-like structure.

The European Hop-hornbeam (*Ostrya carpinifolia*), a tree some 18 metres (60 feet) tall, is native to southern Europe and Asia Minor, and has a broad crown of oval leaves rounded at the base, dark glossy green above, paler beneath and sparsely hairy. The fruit is a hanging, hop-like bunch of about fifteen bladders, each containing a nutlet. These bunches, spread through the crown, shining greenish white, make a fine sight in late summer and autumn. The wood has much the same properties as that of hornbeam.

The American Eastern Hop-hornbeam (*Ostrya virginiana*), like the European species, grows to 18 metres (60 feet) tall and ranges from Nova Scotia through southern Canada to South Dakota and all the eastern states from the Atlantic to Nebraska and south to Texas. The leaves tend to be heart shaped at the base, instead of rounded, and have glandular hairs on their stalks. The nutlets, too, are bigger than those of the European tree. The trees being small and isolated among other species, the timber is rarely exploited.

The Japanese Hop-hornbeam (*Ostrya japonica*), found throughout Japan as well as in Korea and central China, also reaches about 18 metres (60 feet) in height, but has rather longer, more pointed leaves with more hairy undersides than the other two. The timber is highly prized in Japan for furniture and flooring.

GENUS *Corylus* hazels
(the Greek name for hazel)

A genus of fifteen species of deciduous trees and bushes from the northern temperate regions which have the male and female flowers on the same tree, the males in catkins which remain naked on the branches all winter, and the females entirely enclosed in buds with only the pink styles protruding. The seed is enclosed in a hard shell which is itself enveloped in a husk with toothed margins.

Each pair of Hornbeam nuts is attached to the base of a three-lobed wing.

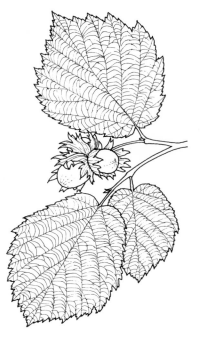

The harshly hairy leaves and nuts of the Common Hazel.

Only two of the hazels can really be called trees. One is the Turkish Hazel (*Corylus colurna*), a native of south-eastern Europe and Asia Minor, which can reach 24 metres (80 feet) in height and girth up to 2·1 metres (7 feet). It is a stately tree, remarkable in this genus, with a fine, conic crown and dark-brown, scaly bark. The leaves are broadly oval with pointed tips and the nuts are larger than the Common Hazel but just as edible. Indeed, the tree is a source of food and timber and a valuable ornamental, too. The other species is the Chinese Hazel (*Corylus chinensis*) which is so similar that many authorities consider it to be a variety of the Turkish tree, although the leaves are less markedly heart shaped at the base. It is found all along the Himalayas into western China.

The Turkish Hazel is often a big tree as much as 24 metres (80 feet) tall.

Above
The lambs' tail male catkins of the Hazel transfer their pollen to the pink female flowers.

Below right
The deeply veined leaves of the Raoul, a deciduous southern beech from Chile.

Far right
The Roble, another southern beech from Chile, grows quickly to reach 30 metres (100 feet) and more in height.

Top
The fifteen- to eighteen-veined, oval leaves of the Raoul.
Bottom
The small, shiny leaves of the Silver Beech.

The Common Hazel (*Corylus avellana*), a native of all parts of Europe south of latitude 68 degrees North, and of Asia Minor, is rarely more than a bush. It is well known in hedgerows and oakwoods where, in southern England, it was cultivated as coppice and its pliant rods were made into hurdles, hoops, and many other products.

Family Fagaceae
GENUS *Nothofagus* southern beeches
(from *nothos*, false and *fagus*, beech)

A genus of some twenty species of sometimes deciduous but usually evergreen, large- to medium-sized trees native to South America and Australasia. The leaves are often very small and the male flowers are usually solitary, or rarely in twos or threes. But, in addition to these small identifying features, the southern beeches, with their small leaves set closely together on shorter stalks, look quite different to the beeches proper. The fruit is a nut completely or partially enclosed in a husk or cup.

The Antarctic Beech (*Nothofagus antarctica*) is a native of a narrow strip along the Chile/Argentine border from Tierra del Fuego some 1950 kilometres (1200 miles) north. It is deciduous and at low elevations attains a large size, up to 30 metres (100 feet) tall, with a broad crown of somewhat twisted branches bearing a dense mass of crumpled, matt-green leaves. Associated with this tree but generally growing at lower altitudes and often taller, up to 39 metres (130 feet), is the Lenga (*Nothofagus pumilo*), also deciduous with glossy, sticky young shoots, and the Oval-leafed Southern Beech (*Nothofagus betuloides*) which is a large, evergreen tree with small, round leaves, speckled with white dots and often with pink veins. In the north of this range, the Coigue (*Nothofagus dombeyi*) is another very large, evergreen tree sometimes as much as 39 metres (130 feet) tall and with dark-green leaves minutely dotted with black specks. A companion species of the Coigue south of Santiago is the Roble (*Nothofagus obliqua*), a fine tree, up to 30 metres (100 feet) tall with smooth, rather pointed, dark-green, deciduous leaves that are paler on the undersides, and with seven to eleven very impressed veins. The Raoul (*Nothofagus procera*), which is otherwise a similar tree in many respects, has larger leaves with smoother margins and fifteen to eighteen veins and shaped very much like those of the horn-beam. These trees will probably be more and more grown as forest trees in Britain and New Zealand where they are fast growing, reaching some 13·5 metres (45 feet) in fifteen years. They also make attractive ornamentals.

The Australian Beech (*Nothofagus moorei*) is a large tree up to 45 metres (150 feet) tall with large, evergreen, glossy leaves, 50 to 75 millimetres (2 to 3 inches) long. It is native to New South Wales where, at one time, it formed dense, pure forests at about 1200 metres (4000 feet) in the Dividing Range. It is the only member of the genus found in subtropical regions. The Tasmanian Beech (*Nothofagus cunninghami*) is

Moss-covered Silver Beeches, Haast Pass Road, Westland, South Island, New Zealand.

a massive tree, 60 metres (200 feet) tall and sometimes as much as 12 metres (40 feet) in girth, native to the western mountainous districts of the island and forming a large proportion of the forests there. The evergreen leaves are small and almost diamond shaped with very short, downy stalks. The timber, locally called red myrtle, is pink in colour and is used like beech wood for furniture, as indeed is the timber of the other members of the genus. This tree also occurs in a few isolated places in Victoria.

The New Zealand Red Beech (*Nothofagus fusca*) is distributed throughout the North and South Islands, particularly in areas of high rainfall, and grows to a height of 30 metres (100 feet) with sharply toothed, wedge-shaped leaves that are thin in texture with prominent veins. The foliage turns brilliant colours in the autumn, and this feature, combined with its slow growth, make it a popular garden tree in New Zealand. The Silver Beech (*Nothofagus menziesii*) is more a tree of the mountains and dry rocky soils up to 900 metres (3000 feet) throughout the country. In young trees and in the upper branches of old trees the bark is silvery grey. The leaves are only 13 millimetres ($\frac{1}{2}$ inch) long, smaller then the Red Beech, shiny, dark green, with rounded teeth on the margins. The timber is deep red and makes attractive furniture. The Black Beech (*Nothofagus solandri*) is a tree of both lowland and hilly areas throughout the country, except in the extreme north of North Island. It has round, blunt, evergreen leaves and black bark when old but it is rarely more than 24 metres (80 feet) tall. The closely related Mountain Beech (*Nothofagus cliffortioides*) found between 600 and 1200 metres (2000 and 4000 feet) in most mountainous areas, has pointed leaves with very hairy short stalks. It seldom exceeds 15 metres (50 feet) in height.

Southern beech forests of one species or another were once a feature of New Zealand with the same bare forest floor that is so typical of beech woods in Europe; but over the years exploitation has greatly reduced them, and even where cut-over areas are left to regenerate naturally, conifers, such as the Totara, tend to come in at the expense of the beech.

GENUS *Fagus* beeches
(the Latin name for a beech tree)

A genus of ten large, deciduous trees, found throughout the northern temperate regions with thin, pointed buds, smooth, grey bark, and large, flat leaves. The male and female flowers are on the same tree, the former in bunches on slender, hanging stalks and the latter in clusters of two or three each producing two nuts enclosed in a four-lobed, woody husk.

The Common Beech (*Fagus sylvatica*) is a native of all Europe between north Scandinavia and Bulgaria and is one of the most handsome and stately of forest trees. Heights of 30 metres (100 feet) are common, and some close-grown trees can top 45 metres (150 feet). Open-grown trees have huge lower branches spreading vastly and carrying dense crowns of

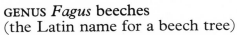
Fagus

114

Overleaf
The Copper Beech contrasts sharply with the greens of neighbouring trees.

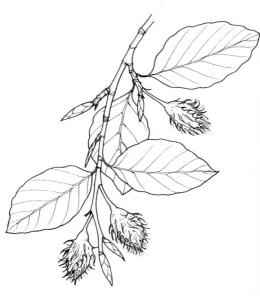

The smooth, oval leaves, the pointed buds, and prickly fruits of the Common Beech.

Left
Tall Beeches at Slindon, Sussex, England, showing the smooth, grey bark and the delicate green of the new season's leaves.

Below
The soft, downy young leaves of the Beech in early May.

The Japanese *Lithocarpus edulis* is a smaller tree, some 18 metres (60 feet) tall but one which is extensively planted in its native Kyushu for its timber, used for fuel, and its edible acorns. The leaves are small and leathery, deep green and lustrous above and covered with dense, brownish scales beneath. The tree is also widely planted as an ornamental in the warmer parts of Japan.

Like the *Chrysolepis*, there are great numbers of species of this genus in tropical and subtropical Asia.

GENUS *Quercus* oaks
(Latin name for the oak tree)

A genus of more than 800 species and hybrids of deciduous and ever-green trees with leaves of various shapes and sizes, but common in their production of acorns – an egg-shaped nut the lower portion of which is enclosed in a cup covered with woody scales. They are found in all north-temperate regions and in tropical and subtropical Asia.

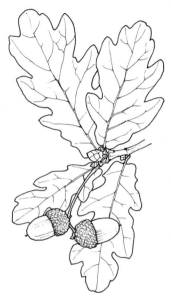

Quercus

No tree is as much loved or held in greater respect by the English as the English Oak (*Quercus robur*), over which they hold proprietory rights despite its wide geographical range well beyond their island limits, from Ireland south to Spain and North Africa and from Russia into south-west Asia. But in lowland Britain, it has dominated the countryside since the dawn of history and played a very special part in that history itself. It was the dominant tree in the great forests which once covered much of southern Britain and many ancient individuals still stand in remnants of these forests. The strong, durable timber, long since recognized as a symbol of sturdy reliability, was the ultimate in building material before steel girders were developed and it is still much prized for fine-quality joinery. The 'wooden walls' of Britain, the ships if the Royal Navy, were built of Oak timber and owed their excellence to it. And in medieval times, the swine herds of England were turned into the Oak forests to feast upon the annual crop of acorns. Kings hid in these trees, felons hung from them, boundaries were marked by them: they are as old as time and part of England.

The short-stalked leaves and the long-stalked acorns of the English or Pedunculate Oak.

The English Oak needs no description except to help distinguish it from a very near relation, the Durmast Oak (*Quercus petrea*), which takes its place in north-west Britain and in upland areas, as well as in other parts of its range. The leaves of the English Oak have two small, ear-like lobes at the base where they join the very short stalk; the Durmast's leaves have long stalks, a tapered base, and no lobes. The

The acorn cups of the Turkey Oak are covered with a mossy coat of downy scales.

acorns of the English species are borne on long stalks usually in pairs, whereas those of the Durmast are stalkless on the branches in groups of two to six. Unfortunately, the two species hybridize, and there are many intermediate forms.

The Turkey Oak (*Quercus cerris*) is also a magnificent tree from southern Europe and south-west Asia but it is much planted and self-seeding in northern Europe including Britain. It is a tall tree, up to 36 metres (120 feet), with leaves much more deeply cut, sometimes almost down to the midrib, by lobes, and with persistent whiskers on the buds and the bases of the leaf stalks. The acorn cup, too, is covered with a mossy coat of downy scales. The Hungarian Oak (*Quercus frainetto*) from Italy, the Balkans, and Hungary is also a stately tree up to 30 metres (100 feet) tall with large, much-lobed leaves as many as ten on each side, unlike any other European oak. Mirbeck's Oak (*Quercus canariensis*), from Spain and North Africa, is another large, handsome species often over 30 metres (100 feet) tall, remarkable for the way its very large, regularly toothed leaves stay on the tree until after Christmas, most of them remaining green until they fall early in the year. The Holm Oak (*Quercus ilex*) is, however, evergreen and a native of the Mediterranean region, where it grows up to 27 metres (90 feet) with a huge, dark, spreading crown of dark-green, glossy leaves, which unfold silvery white and hairy, and very variable in shape: usually oval with smooth margins but often, especially in young trees, with spiky teeth like Holly leaves. The tree is often planted outside its range, particularly in England, as an ornamental, usually singly but sometimes in avenues. The other evergreen species is the Cork Oak (*Quercus suber*), with the same natural range, but a smaller tree, up to 18 metres (60 feet) tall with more consistent oval leaves and spine-tipped lobes. But the remarkable bark is its chief characteristic; it is some 75 millimetres (3 inches) thick, divided into ridges interspersed with deep fissures, and is the chief source of cork. In Portugal, the centre of the industry, the bark is stripped from the trunk every ten years or so without any detriment to the trees, some of which have put up with the treatment for nigh on 500 years.

The American Oaks, which number more than fifty species, are divided into two groups: the white oaks which have acorns ripening in the first year and more or less rounded lobes on their leaves; and the black oaks which have bristle-tipped lobes on their leaves and acorns which ripen in the second year.

The largest of the first group is the White Oak (*Quercus alba*) a tree of the eastern and southern United States, from Maine to Florida and from the Great Lakes to Texas. The up-swept branches support a rounded crown of deeply cut leaves, the lobes being narrow and finger-like. Trees of 45 metres (150 feet) in height and 600 years old have been reported. The timber has many uses and all the properties of oak timber the world over. Taller than the White Oak, but not so majestic in overall size, is the Burr Oak (*Quercus macrocarpa*), ranging over half the United States and parts of Canada, from Saskatchewan to Quebec and south in a broad wedge to Texas. It is the most common oak of the prairie states and the tree can exceed 45 metres (150 feet) in height in parts of Indiana and Illinois. The leaves, the largest of the American oaks and as much as 0·3 metre (1 foot) long, are lobed, round tipped and wedge shaped at the base. The acorns are also large, more than half surrounded by a mossy cup. The Post Oak (*Quercus stellata*) is a smaller tree, usually about 18 metres (60 feet) tall, with a more southerly and eastern distribution, from New England to Kansas and from Florida to Texas, and found growing on widely different sites from rocky ridges to wet bottomlands. The leaves are somewhat leathery with five lobes,

Left
In Portugal the bark is stripped from Cork Oaks every ten years without any apparent detriment to the trees.

Above
The evergreen Holm Oak, a native of the Mediterranean area, is planted in many countries as an ornamental.

The smooth-margined, evergreen leaves of the mature Holm Oak.

123

the middle two the largest and opposite one another. The timber is inclined to be small, unsuitable for sawing and, thus, is used for fencing, hence, presumably the name.

The Live Oak (*Quercus virginiana*) is a massive evergreen tree and a typical feature of the lower coastal plain of the south-eastern United States. Although the trees never attain a great height, seldom more than 18 metres (60 feet), in Louisiana and Mississippi their short boles of up to 6·6 metres (22 feet) in girth support great, spreading crowns 45 metres (150 feet) across, festooned with mosses amid the little, dark-green, glossy leaves. Many of these giants are now protected although they are not as old or as irreplacable as they look. One tree with a spread of 36 metres (120 feet) was found to be only sixty-seven years old.

On the western side the Oregon White Oak (*Quercus garryana*) is found in the humid Pacific coast zone from British Columbia to California and from sea-level to 1200 metres (4000 feet) reaching its maximum development around the Washington/Oregon border, where trees of up to 30 metres (100 feet) tall are found, usually mixed with Douglas Fir and the other conifer giants. The leaves are traditionally oak-shaped and the acorns are very sweet and much sought after by deer and other wildlife. It is the only timber-producing oak on the north-west coast, so that the wood is in demand for furniture, barrels, and cabinet work. The Californian White Oak (*Quercus lobata*) is confined to that state and to the low valleys and plateaux between the Sierra Nevada and the Pacific Ocean. It is a medium-sized tree, seldom taller than 23 metres (75 feet), with small, deeply lobed leaves which are hairy on both sides, a device to protect them from the frequent drying winds. This tree prefers good soils and much of its natural range has been converted to agriculture, so that old specimens are scarce. The brittle timber has few uses other than for fuel.

The evergreen species from the west are the Canyon Live Oak (*Quercus chrysolepis*) and the Californian Live Oak (*Quercus agrifolia*). The former is a small tree, only 15 metres (50 feet) tall, found mainly in the canyons of the coastal ranges of central California and on the foothills of the Sierra Nevada up to 2700 metres (9000 feet). It has thick, yellow-green, leathery leaves and stemless acorns. The latter is a bigger tree with a more southerly range, often semiprostrate on the coastal sand-dunes south of San Francisco, yet sometimes 27 metres (90 feet) tall in the valleys of the coastal ranges in Lower California. The leaves are broader than the canyon species, very much resembling Holly leaves, and the acorns are long and pointed. The wood of both species is hard and heavy and was previously used for agricultural implements and wagon wheels.

Of the second group of American oaks, the Black Oak (*Quercus velutina*) is widespread in the east from Maine to Ontario and from Florida to Louisiana, on drier sites than the White Oak, and reaches heights of 45 metres (150 feet). The leaves are very variable in shape with deep indentations in the margins, some lobes wide and rounded, others finger-like, but all tipped with a bristle. The acorns have little or no stem and are bitter and inedible.

The Red Oak (*Quercus borealis*) is a conspicuous feature in the entire north-east and into eastern Canada where its broad, symmetrical crown on a short bole with spreading branches and dark-green leaves with unequal, bristle-tipped lobes, turn deep orange-red in the autumn. The acorns are reddish brown and almost round, sitting in flat, saucer-like cups. The Scarlet Oak (*Quercus coccinea*) has a similar distribution but is a more slender tree, the ascending branches forming a less billowing crown. The leaves, also very varied in shape, but with fewer bristle-tipped lobes, are shiny on both sides and turn bright scarlet in the autumn, persisting very late in the season. Both these trees grow to about 24 metres (80 feet) tall and their timber, although inferior to the White Oak's, is used for construction purposes and cheap furniture. The third species of eastern and central North American oak which turns red in the autumn is the Pin Oak (*Quercus palustris*). It has a more limited range than the other two, being confined to wet sites in the middle Atlantic states through to Carolina and Arkansas, where it rarely exceeds 24 metres (80 feet) in height with a lightly branched, tall, straight trunk. The leaves are smaller and the lobes very deep, almost to the midrib, and very noticeably bristled; they turn crimson in the autumn. The acorns are very small and a good distinguishing feature.

The Scarlet Oak is one of several species of trees which contribute to the wonderful colours in the north-east American fall.

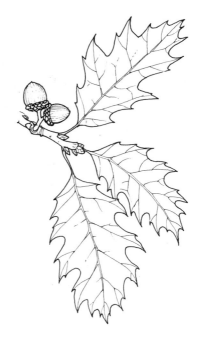

The bristle-tipped leaves of the Red Oak.

This tree is cultivated more as a street and ornamental tree than for its timber which is of little commercial importance.

One of the most attractive black oaks outside the autumn colour season is the Willow Oak (*Quercus phellos*), whose long, narrow, lance-shaped leaves are totally different from its near relatives. It is native in the bottomlands along the coastal plain from Long Island to Georgia, Florida, and eastern Texas. On good sites it can reach 39 metres (130 feet) but is usually about half that height with a domed crown of feathery, vivid-green leaves.

The long, narrow leaves of the Willow Oak give it a more open crown, especially in spring.

The crown of an English Elm in winter has a singular, smoky appearance and is a typical feature of southern England.

Ulmus

Top
The slightly asymmetrical leaves of the English Elm.
Bottom
The larger, more asymmetrical leaves of the Wych Elm.

In the north-west the Californian Black Oak (*Quercus kelloggii*) is the handsome representative of the black oak group, which forms groves of considerable extent on the western slopes of the coastal ranges from Oregon south into California. Some of the finest trees are found at altitudes of 1800 metres (6000 feet) in sheltered valleys where they attain heights of 30 metres (100 feet) or more. The leaves are thick and lustrous, and a dark yellow-green; the egg-shaped acorns are carried on short, thick stalks. It is the biggest oak in that part of the country but the wood is brittle and, in an area where huge conifer timbers are so abundant, is used only for fuel.

One of the commonest trees in northern Japan is the Daimyo Oak (*Quercus dentata*). It is also found in Korea and China. Compared to most other oaks, it is a small tree, seldom more than 18 metres (60 feet) tall, but its leaves are enormous, shaped like the English Oak but up to 0·3 metre (1 foot) long. The round acorns are set in hairy cups. With the same distribution is Oriental White Oak (*Quercus aliena*). It is also a small tree and differs from the Daimyo in having toothed, chestnut-like leaves and egg-shaped acorns in a smooth cup. The Chestnut Oak (*Quercus acutissima*) is somewhat similar of leaf, and spreads westwards right across China into the Himalayas and is a questionable native of Japan but common enough there near villages in the south. It has narrower leaves with more pointed teeth, which are used as food for silkworms.

In the cool, temperate parts of Japan, and in north-east Asia *Quercus mongolica* is a noble forest tree, often growing in pure stands and reaching 30 metres (100 feet) in height. Again, the leaves are toothed rather than lobed but the timber resembles the English species and is in great demand on the world market for furniture and flooring.

The Japanese Evergreen Oak (*Quercus acuta*) is a large tree up to 24 metres (80 feet) tall belonging to the groups of Asiatic oaks which have acorn cups formed of concentric rings rather than separate, joined scales. It is found in the warmer parts of southern Japan and Korea at higher altitudes than other evergreen species. The leaves are dark green above and yellow-brown beneath; they are oblong with long, wavy tips, forming a beautiful, distinctive crown. The well-figured wood has many uses. Also evergreen with similar acorn cups is the Bamboo-leaved Oak (*Quercus myrsinaefolia*) of much the same size and distribution. The leaves are narrower, glossy green above and bluish green beneath, and the acorns are very small, barely 6·4 millimetres ($\frac{1}{4}$ inch) long, and bunched together.

Accustomed as we are to thinking of oaks as trees of temperate climates, it comes as a surprise to learn that there are at least twenty-six species of oaks to be found in the tropical jungles of south-east Asia. They are all evergreen trees, some of them as tall as 45 metres (150 feet), but most of them much smaller. The Singapore Oak (*Quercus conocarpa*), a medium-sized tree some 18 metres (60 feet) tall, is common on the island and less frequent on the peninsula. It has small, dark, glossy green leaves upturned at the edges and with silvery undersides; the acorn is cone-shaped in a shallow, concentric-ringed cup. It is planted mainly to give much-needed shade. Another species, Maingay's Oak (*Quercus maingayi*), found mainly in the mountains of the Malay Peninsula, has large, leathery leaves and gigantic, pear-shaped acorns 64 millimetres ($2\frac{1}{2}$ inches) long and completely enclosed in the cup. None of these tropical oaks has been grown commercially which is surprising because some of them are fine trees.

Family Ulmaceae
GENUS *Ulmus* elms
(Latin name for elm)

A genus of about twenty mostly large, deciduous trees from northern temperate regions west of the Rockies and south of the Himalayas, with small, perfect (bisexual) flowers which come out before the leaves. The fruit is a flat, membranous semitransparent disc (or **samara**) with the seed enclosed in a cavity in the centre or towards the apex.

The English Elm (*Ulmus procera*) is native only to England from the Midlands south-west to Cornwall where, in many parts, it is the dominant hedgerow tree and a typical feature of the English countryside. It is a huge tree, often 36 metres (120 feet) tall and 6 metres (20 feet) in girth, with the straight, unforked trunk bearing great upswept branches and

The lop-sided leaves and the fruit of the Wych Elm.

masses of sprouts emanating from burrs. The twigs at the ends of the branches are slender and curled, giving the crown a singular smoky appearance in winter. The oval leaves, which appear after the reddish tufts of flowers, are dark green with double-toothed margins and are rough to touch on the upper sides which have ten to twelve veins. The leaf blade is bigger on one side than the other. The seeds, in a rounded membrane, are usually sterile and the tree reproduces itself by extensive suckering. The durable timber, which has beauty of colour and grain, is used for furniture, building facings, and coffins. Sadly, this tree is a ready victim of Dutch elm disease, a fungal infection carried by beetles, which clogs up the water vessels and kills first the crown and then the whole tree. Great devastation has already been caused to Elms in the Severn Valley and many other parts of England. With no cure or effective treatment in sight, the future of Britain's Elms seems uncertain.

The Wych Elm (*Ulmus glabra*) is a native of northern and central Europe, including Britain, especially north from Yorkshire and of western Asia. It is a much broader tree than the English species with a more branching trunk and bigger leaves with seventeen or so pairs of veins, even more asymmetrical and more pointed at the tip. The bark, too, differs by remaining quite smooth until well into old age when it becomes ridged. It does not produce suckers from the roots like the English Elm. The Weeping Elm (often seen in parks and gardens) is the 'Camperdown' cultivar of the Wych Elm, usually consisting of a straight bole of the type tree with a head of the drooping, sinuous shoots and the large leaves of the cultivar grafted on the top.

The Smooth-leaved Elm (*Ulmus carpinifolia*) is the species of continental Europe as well as eastern England, North Africa, and western Asia. It is a large tree over 30 metres (100 feet) tall, with a rather narrow habit and branches ascending steeply from the trunk but arching over and ending up with the same slender, curly twigs as the English Elm. The leaves are smaller and more pointed and have smooth, shiny upper surfaces. Two varieties of this tree are locally quite common. The Cornish Elm (*U.c. cornubiensis*) occurs in Cornwall and western Devon. It has even smaller leaves, and branches which leave the trunk at an angle of 45 degrees giving it the shape of a vase, so that it is suitable for roadside planting. The Wheatley Elm (*U.c. sarnienis*), native to the Channel Islands and much planted along by-passes and highways in Britain, has rounder leaves and maintains a regular and well-branched conic shape into relative old age, with the top-most branches almost parallel to the main stem.

There is a group of hybrids between the Wych Elm and the Smooth-leaved Elm which are severally called the Dutch Elm (*Ulmus* x *hollandica*). They are confined to southern England and the eastern Midlands, and have open, thin crowns of big, twisting branches bearing oval leaves which are smooth on top with pointed tips. The Huntingdon Elm, cultivar 'Vegeta', is, like the type tree, a very vigorous grower with long, straight branches radiating out from a short bole at acute angles to form a spreading crown.

The upright habit of the Wheatley Elm makes it a favourite for street and roadside planting.

The curious growth of the Caucasian Elm's branches gives it a unique, flame-like outline.

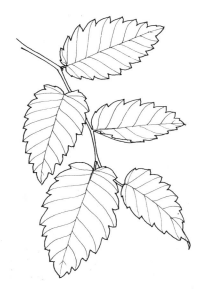

Leaves of the Caucasian Elm.

The American Elm (*Ulmus americana*) is found throughout eastern North America from Nova Scotia to Saskatchewan and from Florida to Texas. It is typically a vase-shaped tree, usually branching low down on the trunk but, even so, often reaching 36 metres (120 feet) in height. The rough, broad, sharp-pointed, lop-sided leaves which have sharply toothed margins, like all elms, appear after the samara, beautifully fringed with pale hairs in this species, have ripened their seeds which germinate immediately. The tree produces no great quantity of suckers. The timber is used for flooring and furniture and, being tough, it was once made into wheel hubs. The Slippery Elm (*Ulmus rubra*) has a similar distribution but not so far north nor south. It is not so graceful or so large as the other species, and is usually about 24 to 27 metres (80 or 90 feet) tall. The crown is broad and the bark is very thick, the inner layer being white, muscilaginous (hence the name), and aromatic as well, resulting, in days gone by, in its being chewed for its thirst-quenching properties and its soothing effect. The leaf buds are hairy, unlike those of the American Elm which are smooth, and the leaves, which are bigger, have extremely rough upper surfaces. Both species have suffered severely from Dutch elm disease, imported from Europe, to the extent that all hope of checking it has been abandoned. America's elms in the east are fast disappearing. Even the Rock Elm (*Ulmus thomasi*), a species with a natural distribution centred west of Lake Michigan, is threatened. This tree usually has a single, straight trunk and a narrow crown of small branches and twigs with two corky wings.

The Japanese Elm (*Ulmus japonica*), also found in Korea, Manchuria and northern China, is a large, broad-crowned tree with pendant branches and corky twigs. The leaves are lop-sided and oblong with toothed margins and rough upper surfaces. The samara are tapered at the base and notched at the top. The tree, which grows to 30 metres (100 feet) tall, is found in pure stands in central and northern Japan as well as in mixture with Katsura trees and maples. The timber is used for building and furniture.

The Chinese Elm (*Ulmus parvifolia*) and the Siberian Elm (*Ulmus pumila*) are both very similar trees from north-eastern Asia, the former also spreading to Japan. Small in comparison with other elms, they rarely reach more than 18 metres (60 feet) in height. The leaves of the former are asymmetrical as usual, but those of the latter are almost equal at the base; the Chinese species flowers in the autumn, the Siberian in the spring.

GENUS *Zelkova*
(from a Caucasian native name)

A genus of five species of deciduous trees from the Caucasus and eastern Asia closely allied to the elms but differing from them in having uni-sexual flowers both on the same twig, and bearing stalked nutlets on the twigs.

The Caucasian Elm (*Zelkova carpinifolia*) is a native of the Caucasus Mountains. It has a very short, smooth-barked, stout bole bearing a great number of small, upright-growing branches providing a unique, flame-like shape sometimes nearly 27 metres (90 feet) tall. The leaves are oval and slightly heart shaped at the base and, as the name implies, somewhat like those of the Hornbeam. In the autumn they turn an orange-brown. The timber is tough and durable but unknown in commerce.

The Keaki (*Zelkova serrata*) is a native of Japan, Korea, Manchuria, and northern China. In Japan it is one of the largest and most important trees growing along streams and at the foot of mountains where it can reach 39 metres (130 feet) in height. The leaves have markedly toothed margins and are more slender and pointed than the Caucasian species. The timber is of great value in Japan for boat building, construction work, and furniture, and the Keaki is much planted there as a street tree as well as in shelter belts. It is excellent for bonzai work. The Chinese Zelkova (*Zelkova sinica*) is a much smaller tree, not more than 18 metres (60 feet) tall, but otherwise very similar except that its bark shows more of the orange colour because it flakes more freely, and the leaves are not quite so long and pointed.

The Keaki from Japan, where it is a large tree, is also a favourite species for bonzai work.

GENUS *Celtis* hackberries, nettle-trees
(the Greek name for an unrelated but similar tree)

A genus of some seventy mostly deciduous trees and shrubs from North America, south-east Europe, subtropical Africa and Asia, China, and Japan. They differ from the elms, to which they are closely related, in having leaves with three main nerves rising from the base instead of one, and their fruits being round and fleshy like a cherry.

The Nettle-tree (*Celtis australis*), a native of the Mediterranean area and south-west Asia, is a medium-sized, round-topped tree with grey bark like a beech. Sometimes, it is as tall as 21 metres (70 feet) but it is more often rather shrubby. The leaves which are wedge shaped, have long tapering points and are very rough on their upper surfaces. The reddish-brown, round fruits, about 13 millimetres ($\frac{1}{2}$ inch) in diameter, are borne on long stalks. The strong, elastic timber is used locally for tool handles and agricultural implements, and the foliage is often lopped as cattle and goat fodder in the drier part of the tree's range. It is planted as a street tree in some cities in southern Europe but consistently fails to grow in Britain.

The White Stinkwood (*Celtis africanus*) is one of the most widely distributed of South Africa's native trees. It is found growing from sea-level up to 2100 metres (7000 feet) throughout the eastern part of the country as far north as Ethiopia. According to the site, it varies in size from no more than a shrub to a tree 24 metres (80 feet) tall, with a straight, clean, pale grey bole. In spring, the simple, three-veined leaves have a green freshness seldom seen in the foliage of other native trees. The yellow-brown berries are relished by birds. The timber, when freshly cut, has an unpleasant smell, and has a long grain and woolly texture; it is used for yokes, planking, and sometimes for furniture.

The Hackberry (*Celtis occidentalis*) is widely distributed in the eastern United States and Canada where it is usually a small tree about 15 metres (50 feet) tall, often growing quite isolated from others of its kind. In the lower Mississippi valley where it attains its maximum development, it is sometimes over 30 metres (100 feet) tall. The leaves are broader than the Nettle-tree's but have the tapering points; and the purple, cherry-like fruits remain on the tree all winter as a welcome reserve food supply for birds. The timber is used for crates, boxes, and furniture. The Sugarberry (*Celtis laevigata*) has a more southerly range into Florida, the Gulf States, and even Bermuda. It is a smaller tree, again very often a bush, but sometimes 24 metres (80 feet) tall, with rounder leaves without the tapering points. The fruit is orange-red and readily consumed by birds. Both these species, because of their wide distribution and consequent tolerance of differing soils, are popular as shade and ornamental trees.

From Japan, Korea, and northern China is *Celtis sinensis*, a tree some 21 metres (70 feet) tall with deep-green, toothed leaves and orange-green fruits, the stones of which are sculptured in a net-like pattern. It grows along river banks and damp places and is a popular roadside tree in Japan. The fruits are sweet enough to attract children and the wood is used for kitchen utensils and for fuel.

Several evergreen species of *Celtis* occur in Sri Lanka, the Philippines, and some Pacific islands. Some of them are large trees up to 30 metres (100 feet) tall.

Family Moraceae
GENUS *Morus* mulberries
(Latin name for a mulberry)

A genus of twelve species of medium-sized deciduous trees from the temperate and subtropical regions of the Northern Hemisphere. The leaves are toothed and usually broadly oval and sometimes lobed. The flowers are normally unisexual, borne on hanging catkins, and the fruit is a cluster of succulent drupes resembling a large blackberry, but botanically quite different.

The Black Mulberry (*Morus nigra*) has been cultivated in Europe and elsewhere for so long that the exact location of its Asiatic origin is lost in the mists of time. It seldom exceeds 9 metres (30 feet) in height with a short bole, twisting branches, large, heart-shaped leaves up to 150 millimetres (6 inches) long, which are deep green, rough and hairy

The Black Mulberry has been cultivated in Europe for so long that its exact Asian place of origin is unknown.

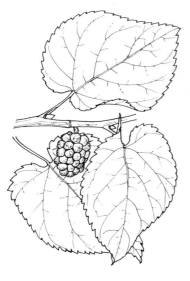

Leaves and succulent, purple fruit of the Black Mulberry.

above, and paler beneath. The fruit, red to start with but turning dark purplish just before falling, has an agreeable sweet/sour flavour.

The Red Mulberry (*Morus rubra*) is a native of eastern and central United States where it grows up to 18 metres (60 feet) tall with a dense, round crown of rather smaller, heart-shaped leaves with a prominent, orange-coloured midrib on the downy underside. The red fruit also darkens to a purple before falling and is valued for fattening pigs and poultry. This tree does not grow well in Europe. Another species, the Mexican Mulberry (*Morus microphylla*) which is found in the canyons of the Colorado valley in Texas and south into Mexico, has much smaller leaves, barely 38 millimetres (1½ inches) long although it, too, reaches 18 metres (60 feet) in height on good sites. The fruit is similar to the red species.

Ficus

The White Mulberry (*Morus alba*) is a native of China but has been cultivated for centuries in much of temperate Asia and in south-eastern Europe. It is very similar tree to the black species but it tends to be narrower of habit, and the leaves are shiny, not rough, above and a paler green. The fruit starts white, turning yellowish or sometimes pink before falling. The leaves of this species are the main food of the silkworm and have been cultivated for this purpose for centuries. The tree is also planted as a street tree in south-east Europe where the old, rugged trunks blend well with cobbled market places.

GENUS *Maclura*
(after William Maclure, an American geologist)

A genus of a single species of medium-sized, deciduous trees with spiny twigs, oval leaves, and insignificant flowers borne on separate male and female trees. The fruits are large and orange shaped, and yellow-green in colour.

The Osage Orange (*Maclura pomifera*) is sometimes 18 metres (60 feet) tall and is a tree of the rich bottom lands of Arkansas, Oklahoma, and south to Texas. It has orange-coloured bark and shiny leaves which turn bright yellow in the autumn. The remarkable fruits, borne high up in the female trees, are like warty skinned, semiripe, dried-up oranges, about 130 millimetres (5 inches) in diameter, and are quite inedible. The tree is much planted for shelter and as hedges in the prairie regions and the timber is very hard, strong, tough, and durable. It was used by the Indians for making bows.

GENUS *Ficus* figs
(the Latin for a fig)

An immense genus of over 600 species of mainly evergreen trees of very varied habit found in tropical and subtropical parts of both hemispheres, and occasionally in warm temperate areas. The flowers are borne inside a hollow receptacle which ultimately swells and becomes the fruit.

The fig of commerce and ancient history is the Common Fig (*Ficus carica*), a native of western Asia and the eastern Mediterranean region. It is a small tree, about 9 metres (30 feet) tall, and a deciduous one, unusual for figs, with broad, lobed leaves of classic shape. The flowers are produced on the inner surfaces of a green, pear-shaped receptacle with a small aperture at the top through which, as is remarkably the case with all species of figs, gall wasps gain entry to lay their eggs. After hatching and mating in the receptacle, the young wasps, covered in pollen from the flowers, emerge and fly off to other figs of the same species to lay their eggs, and in the process fertilize other flowers. The receptacle in the case of the Common Fig later develops into the purple succulent fruit we know as the fig. Each species of fig has its own special gall wasp.

The sycamore of the Bible is *Ficus sycomorus* which is native to North Africa, south through Ethiopia down to the Transvaal and Zululand. In the southern part of its range, it is a huge, spreading tree some 24 metres (80 feet) tall, with a yellowish trunk, heart-shaped leaves about 75 millimetres (3 inches) long and round fruit 25 millimetres (1 inch) in diameter borne in bunches on the branches, and eaten by birds. The Cape Fig (*Ficus capensis*) is also a large, spreading tree found throughout forest areas of South Africa, with large, simple leaves about 150 millimetres (6 inches) long which are sometimes but not always deciduous. The figs are 38 millimetres ($1\frac{1}{2}$ inches) in diameter and are sweet to the taste but so riddled with insects, like all wild figs, that they are unappetizing. The tree is generally planted to give shade, which it does admirably. The Natal Fig (*Ficus natalensis*) belongs to the group of figs known as 'stranglers'. They start life as a seed dropped by a monkey or a bird in a branch crotch or hole in another tree. After germination, some roots will reach down to the ground, take root and spread laterally round the host tree's trunk, gradually enveloping it and slowly crushing it to death, eventually to stand a giant tree in its place. The Natal Fig does this and emerges one of the biggest figs in South Africa, making a wonderful shade tree along the hot Natal coast. One example of the Wonderboom (*Ficus pretoriae*), a species whose branches habitually bend down to the ground and take root forming an ever-

Top
The leaves with drawn-out tips and the little figs of the Peepul.
Bottom
The classic fig leaves and fruits (*above*) and a fig in cross-section (*below*) of the Common Fig.

widening circle of trees, growing near Pretoria, now has a spread of 50 metres (165 feet) and is 23 metres (75 feet) tall. Most of the branches linking the circles have decayed and disappeared leaving a space beneath which over 1000 people can stand. The parent trunk is estimated to be 1000 years old.

Of Asiatic figs, the Banyan (*Ficus benghalensis*) is perhaps the best known. A strangling fig from India, it eventually reaches enormous sizes, up to 30 metres (100 feet) tall with a mass of subsidiary trunks formed from roots giving it the distinction of having the biggest crown of any tree in the world. One near Poona had a measured circumference of 600 metres (2000 feet). Seeds from this tree deposited in cracks in

Far left
The fruits of the Common Fig are green at first, becoming purple and succulent as they ripen.

Below
The Banyan forms subsidiary trunks from roots growing downwards from the branches, eventually giving the tree an enormous spread.

walls and buildings result in trees which sever the masonry and level it to dust. The Peepul (*Ficus religiosa*) is also an Indian tree, normally a strangling species but when planted by the roadside, which it often is, can develop into a fine tree standing on its own trunk. It also reaches 30 metres (100 feet) in height and is regarded with much awe and reverence among Hindus and Buddhists. The leaves are delicately oval shaped, with the tips drawn out into long tails and stalks flattened like the Aspen's causing them to flutter in the gentlest breeze with a rattling sound. They are deciduous but the crown remains bare for only a short while.

The Large-leaved Banyan (*Ficus wightiana*) is found in southern Japan, Taiwan, and southern China where it is a big, spreading tree some 24 metres (80 feet) tall, with large, deep-green, evergreen, shiny leaves and purple-white spotted figs. It is much planted as a street and shade tree. The timber is used for turnery and barrels.

The Australian Silky Oak is planted in many countries as a street tree and also as a shade tree in Indian tea gardens.

GENUS *Antiaris*
(from the Malay name *Antjar*)

A genus of four evergreen, tropical trees from Asia, Africa, and Madagascar with milky white juice in all their parts, and simple leaves. The The male and female flowers are on the same tree, the latter grouped in the leaf axils and producing a small pulpy fruit.

The Upas Tree (*Antiaris toxicaria*), native to southern China, India, and Malaya, is a tall tree 30 metres (100 feet) in height with a stout, tapering trunk bearing a crown of short but spreading branches with oblong leaves. The fruit is pear shaped and velvety red. Legend gave this tree dire and deadly poisonous properties, such as certain death from noxious emanations to men and animals which approached it, and a withering of other plants unlucky enough to grow near it. None is true, but the milky substance which exudes from wounds was used as an arrow poison.

GENUS *Artocarpus*
(from *artos*, bread, *karpos*, fruit)

This is one of the most characteristic genera of the eastern tropics, and contains about fifty species of evergreen trees native to south-east Asia and the Pacific islands. The leaves are large, dark green, and shiny, and the fruits, which range from small to enormous, are formed from the swollen female flower head.

The Breadfruit (*Artocarpus incisus*) is indigenous to the Pacific islands and planted throughout tropical Asia and America. A spreading tree up to 18 metres (60 feet) tall, it has very large leaves 0·6 metre (2 feet) long and deeply cut into several pointed lobes. The round or oblong fruits, hanging from the branches on stout stalks in twos and threes, are as big as footballs and usually rather prickly. The seeds are embedded in the mass of pulp which forms these fruits. Seedless varieties have been developed and the fruit of these, as it softens, is cut into slices and can be boiled, baked, or fried. It can also be dried and ground into flour. The resulting bread is always tough and tasteless but nevertheless is an important food in places where other fare is scarce. To transport some specimens of this tree from Tahiti to the West Indies, as food for slaves, was the object of Captain Bligh's disastrous voyage in H.M.S. *Bounty*. He subsequently succeeded and the tree now flourishes in the Americas.

The Jack Fruit (*Artocarpus heterophyllus*), probably a native of India and grown there as well as throughout south-east Asia, is a tree of similar size and shape but the simple leaves are only about 230 millimetres (9 inches) long, oval, shiny green, and leathery. The huge, pear-shaped fruits which hang from the trunk and main branches are up to 0·9 metre (3 feet) long, weighing as much as 40 kilograms (90 pounds), and with the possible exception of freak marrows or pumpkins, they are the largest fruits known. That the Jack Fruit can grow to 12 metres (40 feet) in three years and start producing fruit at that age, is a measure of the lushness of tropical tree growth.

Family Protoceae
GENUS *Grevillea*
(after C F Greville, a founder member of the Royal Horticultural Society)

A genus of about 170 species of evergreen trees from Australia, New Caledonia, and the New Hebrides. The leaves are deeply toothed or lobed and the fruits are boat-shaped pods containing flat, winged seeds.

The Silky Oak (*Grevillea robusta*), a rainforest species from Queensland and New South Wales, where it grows up to 40 metres (130 feet) tall, has beautiful feathery leaves, often 0·3 metre (1 foot) long, dark green on top but shining, silky white beneath. The orange flowers have long, protruding styles and are arranged on the branches to look like bunches of combs. The attractive, silky grained wood is used for cabinet making but this tree is also planted in many warm, temperate countries outside its natural range for shade and for ornament. In India it is planted to give shade in tea gardens where its feathery crown filters the sunlight on to the bushes; and in South Africa it is planted as a street tree.

The feathery leaves of the Silky Oak.

The Katsura Tree, one of the largest deciduous trees in Japan, turns a beautiful lemon yellow in the autumn.

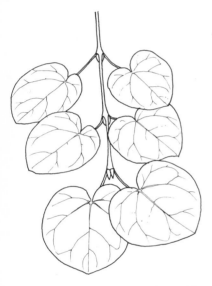

The round leaves, with heart-shaped bases of the Katsura Tree.

The leathery leaves and the big, single flower of the Magnolia.

Family Cercidiphyllaceae
GENUS *Cercidiphyllum*
(*cercis*, Judas tree, *phyllos*, leaf)

A genus of one species of large, deciduous trees from Japan and China, with round leaves emerging opposite to one another on the twigs and male and female flowers on separate trees. The fruits are pods borne in clusters and contain winged seeds.

The Katsura Tree (*Cercidiphyllum japonicum*) is a native of China and Japan, and in the latter country is the largest deciduous tree and one of the most important timber producers, reaching heights of over 30 metres (100 feet) with a remarkably symmetrical, rounded crown of nearly round bluish-green leaves with heart-shaped bases, paler on the undersides, and turning a lovely butter yellow in the autumn, or sometimes orange in young trees. The claw-like pods are held in clusters of two to six on short stalks. The timber is light, soft, and fine grained, and is used for interior work in buildings and for furniture. The beautifully delicate foliage and the variety of autumn colours which it provides have made this tree a very popular ornamental in Britain although it does tend to suffer from late spring frosts.

Family Magnoliaceae
GENUS *Magnolia*
(after Pierre Magnol, a French professor of botany)

A genus of thirty-five species of deciduous and evergreen flowering trees and shrubs from North and Central America, the Himalayas, China, and Japan. They have buds with a single scale, big, simple leaves, and large, solitary flowers which eventually produce a cone-like fruit.

The Southern Magnolia (*Magnolia grandiflora*), with a natural range from south-east Carolina along the Atlantic coast to Florida, and east along the Gulf coast to Texas, is a magnificent, evergreen tree up to 30 metres (100 feet) tall, with large, oval, lustrous-green leaves 150 to 200 millimetres (6 to 8 inches) long, bearing, from April to June in America and from July to November in Europe, large, creamy white, fragrant flowers, 200 millimetres (8 inches) across, with six to twelve wax-like petals. The Southern Magnolia is a fine, free-standing tree in its natural range, and sometimes has a bole of 4·5 metres (15 feet) in girth. It produces a useful commercial timber as well as being planted in parks and gardens where, in Britain, it is more often than not seen as a large, spreading bush planted against a wall.

The Cucumber Tree (*Magnolia acuminata*) is also a large tree extending south from Ontario down the Appalachians and to southern Missouri. Sometimes as tall as 27 metres (90 feet), with sweeping lower limbs touching the ground and the upper branches ascending into a conic crown, it bears sharp-pointed, oblong leaves and, among them, inconspicuous, pale-green flowers eventually turning into 75-millimetre (3-inch) long 'cucumbers' which are green at first and later purplish red.

The Japanese Cucumber Tree (*Magnolia hypoleuca*) is confined to that country and is common in the cool, temperate regions where it grows to about 30 metres (100 feet) tall. The large leaves 460 millimetres (18 inches) long, pale, shiny green above and greyish green below, appear before the white flowers which are 200 millimetres (8 inches) across and strongly scented. The soft, closely grained wood is used for furniture, clogs, and drawing boards. The cone-shaped fruits are brilliant red.

The Northern Japanese Magnolia (*Magnolia kobus*) is native to that country and to Quelpaert Island, south of Korea. It grows to about 18 metres (60 feet) tall and has abruptly pointed, oval leaves that are dark green, slightly wrinkled above and hairy beneath. The rather small [100 millimetres (4 inches) across] white flowers appear before the leaves. The wood is used for matches and charcoal but the tree is much more valued for its spring display of flowers and is extensively planted throughout Japan for this purpose. The fruit is pink, containing red seeds which often hang on threads before finally falling.

The Yulan (*Magnolia denudata*), from central China where it grows up to 15 metres (50 feet) tall, has been cultivated by the Chinese for centuries. It has bell-shaped flowers of pure white which bloom before the leaves. The flowers are often depicted on old porcelain and in ancient paintings. This species has hybridized with another Sino-Japanese

Left
America's Southern Magnolia is often seen as a large bush growing against a wall.

Below
The Hybrid Magnolia's white flowers appear in profusion before the leaves.

Top
Campbell's Magnolia is one of the most magnificent of the group, with its 250-millimetre (10-inch) wide, rosy pink flowers.

Above
The Tulip Tree is one of the largest trees native to eastern North America, often as much as 45 metres (150 feet) tall.

Right
The Tulip Tree's greenish-white flowers are usually hidden among the saddle-shaped leaves high up in the crown.

species, *Magnolia liliflora*, to produce a series of hybrids extensively planted in Europe and called collectively *Magnolia soulangeana*. They produce splendid, white, bell-shaped flowers on the naked shoots at first, but continuing after the leaves have emerged, until June.

Campbell's Magnolia (*Magnolia campbellii*), a native of eastern Nepal, Sikkim, and Bhutan at the eastern end of the Himalayas, is perhaps the most magnificent of the genus. Trees of up to 45 metres (150 feet) tall were quite common a century ago but the demand for timber laid them low, and 24 metres (80 feet) or so is now the largest size. They grow at elevations of between 2400 and 3000 metres (8000 and 10 000 feet), and in April, as they stand leafless but covered with huge, rosy pink, 250-millimetre (10-inch) flowers, among the oaks and birches, they are a remarkable sight. The leaves, which appear later, are shiny light green above and with a downy white tinge below.

GENUS *Liriodendron* tulip trees
(*leirion*, lily, *dendron*, tree)

A genus of two large deciduous trees, one each from North America and China, closely related to the magnolias but differing from them in having truncated, never pointed, leaves and flattened terminal buds with curved tips.

The Tulip Tree (*Liriodendron tulipifera*) is one of the largest trees in the eastern states of America ranging from New England south to Florida and attaining their maximum development in the lower Ohio Valley and in fertile lower parts of the southern Appalachians, where they are 45 metres (150 feet) tall and 7·5 metres (25 feet) in girth; forest-grown trees often have 24-metre (80-foot) trunks clear of branches. The long, stalked leaves are quite unlike any other American tree; they are three-lobed with the central one blunt, as if snipped off with scissors. They turn rich yellow in the autumn. The flowers, produced in

June, are shaped like a small tulip but, being greenish white and borne high up on the tree, are difficult to see and the name leads to disappointment. Nevertheless, the tree is magnificent in both summer and winter with its narrow-domed, columnar crown and is a popular ornamental in large gardens in Britain. The timber is soft and easily worked and is much in demand under the confusing name of yellow poplar.

The Chinese Tulip Tree (*Liriodendron chinense*), from central China, is a smaller tree not recorded as exceeding 18 metres (60 feet) in height, but otherwise almost indistinguishable from the American species except that the leaves are more deeply cut and are paler on the undersides, and the twigs are grey, not shiny brown. This striking example of two species so far removed from one another geographically, yet so alike in almost every respect, emphasizes the interesting fact that a great many tree species in eastern North America have very similar counterparts in China.

The characteristic 'snipped-off' leaves and the flower of the Tulip Tree.

Family Myristicaceae
GENUS *Myristica* nutmegs

A genus of about 120 species of evergreen trees mostly from tropical Asia with oily, evergreen, simple leaves that are oblong, pointed, and leathery. The very small male and female flowers are on separate trees, and the fruits are round with a fleshy outer covering enclosing a single, hard seed, itself surrounded by a pulpy coat.

The Nutmeg (*Myristica fragrans*), long cultivated in south-east Asia, probably originated in New Guinea and the Moluccas where its nearest related species grows naturally. It is a tree up to 18 metres (60 feet) tall and has short, narrow leaves which are coppery brown on the undersides. The fleshy fruit, about the size of an apricot and brown in colour, contains the single seed which, when grated, becomes the nutmeg of the kitchen, and its red waxy covering when dried and powdered becomes mace. Thus, two common spices come from the fruit of a single tree.

Family Lauraceae
GENUS *Cinnamomum* cinnamon and camphor trees
(Greek name for cinnamon)

A genus of about 150 species of evergreen trees with opposite, three-veined, simple leaves, tiny white flowers and 13-millimetre ($\frac{1}{2}$-inch) round, blue-black berries.

The Camphor Tree (*Cinnamomum camphora*) is a large, spreading, aromatic, evergreen tree some 18 metres (60 feet) tall and native to Japan, Taiwan, and southern China. In southern Japan it is one of the most important trees because, not only do its leaves, shoots, bark, and wood chips produce camphor oil when distilled, but its wood is greatly

The evergreen leaves, female flowers, and the fleshy fruit of the Nutmeg Tree.

The Camphor Tree is not only an important ornamental but produces a fragrant timber, and camphor oil is distilled from its leaves and bark.

The leaves of the Bay Laurel were used by the Romans to make crowns for their triumphant heroes.

valued for chests, furniture, and book-cases because of its insect-repelling properties. It is also a very popular ornamental and shade tree, and some of the older and more splendid specimens have been designated as national monuments.

The Cinnamon Tree (*Cinnamomum zeylanicum*), a native of south-west India and Sri Lanka, is a tree some 12 metres (40 feet) tall but with leaves twice the size of the Camphor Tree's – as much as 150 millimetres (6 inches) long. The bark and leaves smell strongly of cinnamon. It is the bark of young shoots, particularly suckers, which, when stripped off and dried, produces the cinnamon of commerce.

GENUS *Laurus* laurels
(Latin name for Bay Laurel)

A genus of two species of evergreen, aromatic trees with simple, shiny leaves. The male and female flowers are borne on separate trees and the fruit is a black berry.

The Bay Laurel (*Laurus nobilis*), a native of the Mediterranean region, is a pyramidal tree some 15 metres (50 feet) tall with dark, glossy green, oval leaves, often with wavy margins. The small, greenish-yellow female flowers produce round, shiny-black fruit about 13 millimetres ($\frac{1}{2}$ inch) in diameter. It is the laurel of the Romans for whose triumphant heroes the leaves were made into crowns; and wreathes of the fruiting sprays were presented to their distinguished poets, hence the name, poet laureate. The tree is often planted in tubs and clipped into formal shapes for decorating the entrances to large hotels and public buildings, especially in continental Europe. The Canary Island Laurel (*Laurus canariensis*), a tree of the same shape and size, is native to those islands and the Azores. It differs from the Bay Laurel in being much less hardy and has larger leaves and downy twigs.

The shiny, evergreen leaves of the Bay Laurel.

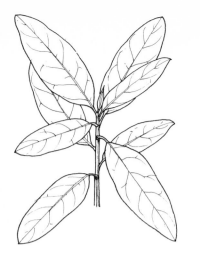

The leaves of the Californian Laurel have a strong, camphor-like, pungent smell.

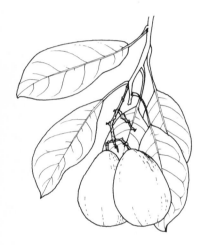

The evergreen leaves and the pear-shaped fruits of the Avocado Pear.

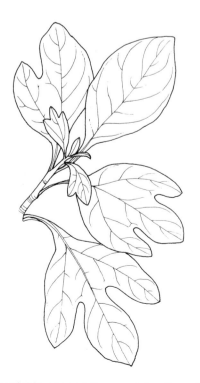

The variable-shaped leaves of the Sassafras.

GENUS *Umbellularia* californian laurels
(bearing flowers in umbels)

A genus of one species of large, evergreen, aromatic trees from north-west America, which differ from the true laurels in having their flowers in spreading bunches or umbels on the ends of the twigs.

The Californian Laurel (*Umbellularia californica*) is a large and very variable tree of the Pacific coast region of north-west America, from Douglas County in Oregon south to San Diego in California on coastal flats and up to 1200 metres (4000 feet) elevation in the coastal mountains. On fertile sites it exceeds 45 metres (150 feet) in height, and when open grown has an impressive, rounded crown of shiny, elliptical leaves. The fruits resemble olives in shape, size, and colour. When crushed, the leaves emit a strong, camphor-like, pungent odour which can cause headaches; indeed, even sitting under one of these trees can result in sneezing and headaches in some people. The timber is hard and heavy and turns beautifully. Paperweights, bowls, candlesticks, and carved figures are made from it and sold under the name of myrtle wood in stalls and gift shops throughout its range.

GENUS *Persea*
(Greek name for an Egyptian tree with sweet fruit)

A genus of 150 species of medium-sized, tropical and subtropical, evergreen trees, mostly from South America, with simple leaves with smooth margins, and perfect flowers giving rise to round or pear-shaped fruits containing a single seed or stone.

The Avocado Pear (*Persea americana*) is about 18 metres (60 feet) tall and a native of Mexico and Central America. The oval leaf is about 150 millimetres (6 inches) long, dark green above and bluish green beneath. The small, fragrant, yellowish flowers are crowded on the ends of branches each producing a 100-millimetre (4-inch) long, pear-shaped, yellowish-green fruit containing an edible and highly nutritious pulp and one large seed. The tree is planted for these fruits in many tropical countries.

GENUS *Sassafras*
(from a North American Indian name)

A genus of three species of large, deciduous trees, native to North America, China, and Taiwan, with lobed leaves and male and female flowers on separate trees.

The Sassafras (*Sassafras albidum*), which ranges over much of eastern North America, from Maine to Florida and from Michigan to Texas, is unusual for a member of the laurel family in being deciduous. On good sites in the Smoky Mountains of North Carolina, it may be as much as 30 metres (100 feet) tall with a broad top and branches at right angles to the trunk. The leaves are variable and unevenly lobed but all have wedge-shaped bases and are shiny pale green in colour, turning yellow to red in the autumn. The fruits are dark blue and berry-like on the ends of long, red stalks. The timber is fragrant and durable but is only used for fencing posts and other farm requirements.

Family Hamamelidaceae
GENUS *Liquidambar* sweet gums
(*liquidus*, liquid, *ambar* (Arabic), amber)

A genus of three species of large, deciduous trees native to south-west Asia, China, and Taiwan, with palmately lobed leaves and spiny, round fruits hanging on long stalks.

The Sweet Gum (*Liquidambar styraciflua*) is native to the south-east of the United States from Connecticut to Florida and Texas, with a variety found in isolated areas of southern Mexico and Guatemala. It can be as tall as 36 metres (120 feet) but frequently forks when it is only about half that height with a wide crown. The star-shaped leaves are rather like those of some maples but are alternative and not opposite and on very long stalks. They turn scarlet and later deep red in the autumn. The fruits are spiky balls 38 millimetres (1½ inches) in diameter which hang on stalks from the bases of the leaf stalks. A winged seed is attached to each spike. The bark exudes a yellow, fragrant liquid like the storax of commerce, and the timber has a beautiful natural grain and is frequently marketed as satin-walnut for furniture and panelling. Few trees in the American south-east can equal this for autumn colours, so it is much planted as an ornamental.

The Chinese Sweet Gum (*Liquidambar formosana*) from China and Taiwan is a smaller tree, 24 metres (80 feet) tall, with leaves that are three lobed instead of five, and have red stalks and purple veins. The Oriental Sweet Gum (*Liquidambar orientalis*), from Asia Minor, is bigger again at 30 metres (100 feet) tall and has smaller leaves with much blunter points on its three to five lobes. This tree is the commercial source of liquid storax, a soft, viscid, aromatic resin which comes from the inner bark. It is said to form the basis of friar's balsam.

GENUS *Parrotia*
(after F W Parrot, a Russian naturalist)

A genus of one species of small, deciduous trees, native to northern Persia and the Caucasus Mountains, with grey, flaky bark, rather like a Plane tree's, thick, dark, glossy green, oval leaves, and flowers in bunches with red stamens which come out before the leaves.

The Persian Ironwood (*Parrotia persica*) is a small tree 9 to 12 metres (30 to 40 feet) tall with a short, stout trunk and arching branches giving a sparse, wide, top. The leaves, which resemble those of the Beech, take on remarkably rich gold and crimson colours in the autumn, and it is chiefly for this reason that the tree is planted in parks and gardens in many parts of Europe.

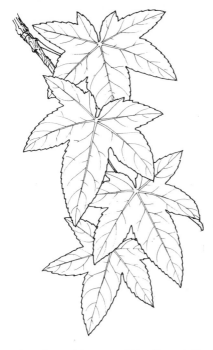

The star-shaped leaves of the Sweet Gum.

Left
Although it is never a large tree, the Persian Ironwood is a fine garden subject with its rich gold and crimson colours in the autumn.

Above
Few trees in the American south-east can equal the Sweet Gum for autumn colours.

The wavy margined leaves of the Persian Ironwood.

145

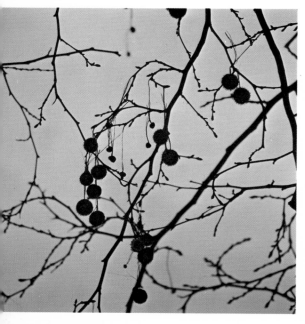

Family Platanaceae
GENUS *Platanus* plane trees
(the Greek name for the Oriental Plane)

A genus of six species of large, deciduous trees, found in North America, Mexico, southern Europe, and western Asia to India, with flaky bark, large, maple-like leaves, and fruits in the form of spherical balls hanging on long, pendulous stalks throughout the winter.

The Oriental Plane (*Platanus orientalis*), native to south-eastern Europe and western Asia, is an immense, spreading tree up to 30 metres (100 feet) tall with a great, domed crown extending over a large area because of the low branches, often so big that they touch the ground. The leaves are smaller than the London Plane with more deeply cut, sharper lobes. The fruits hang two to six on each stalk. This tree is the *Chenar* of the famous Moghul gardens in Kashmir and its leaves are a common motif on carvings from that country. Some magnificent specimens of this very long-lived tree can be seen in Yugoslavia and the Bosporus; and it is mentioned in the Bible on several occasions as a tree to be held in as much awe and respect as the Cedar of Lebanon.

The American Sycamore (*Platanus occidentalis*) or Buttonwood is native throughout the eastern half of the United States from Maine to Nebraska and from northern Florida to Texas. It is the most massive of all broadleaved American trees, often exceeding 42 metres (140 feet) in height and 6 metres (20 feet) in girth; one tree in Indiana measured 51 metres (168 feet) tall and 10 metres (33 feet) in circumference. The leaves, which are often broader than they are long, have three shallow lobes and are sometimes 250 millimetres (10 inches) wide. The fruits hang singly and the mottled bark, typical of the genus, is almost white on the upper trunk and branches. The timber, because it rots quickly outside, is used for boxes, butchers' blocks, and cigar boxes.

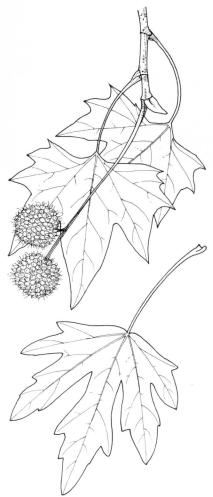

The London Plane (*Platanus* x *hispanicus*) is a hybrid between the Oriental Plane and the American Sycamore which is thought to have arisen in Spain around about 1650. It was first planted in England at Ely and at Barnes about 1680. The fine, old trees are still there. The large, five-lobed leaves are up to 250 millimetres (10 inches) across, the lobes being sharply pointed and much deeper than the American species. The fruits hang three to four on a stalk. These superb trees are a common and well-loved feature of London's squares and gardens, where they frequently grow more than 30 metres (100 feet) tall with flaking, scarcely tapered boles; and they do it very quickly. A tree in central London reached 23 metres (75 feet) in height and over 2·7 metres (9 feet) in girth in fifty-seven years. The tree's ability to thrive in compacted or even tarmac-covered soil, and its resistance to air pollution, combined with its many other attributes, make it ideal for urban planting.

The London Plane is a well-loved feature of London's parks and squares and the trees often reach great sizes.

Family Rosaceae

GENUS *Crataegus* thorn trees
(the Greek name for Hawthorn)

A genus of many hundreds of shrubs, but some trees, found in North America, Europe, and most of temperate Asia. They are deciduous and are armed with thorns which are really modified branches. The five-petalled flowers are borne in flat clusters giving rise to berry-like fruits.

The Hawthorn (*Crataegus monogyna*) is a small tree up to 12 metres (40 feet) tall, native from Europe east to Afghanistan. The dark, shiny leaves have four lobes each side of the midrib and the white, fragrant flowers are borne in dense masses in mid-May, to be followed by dark red 'haws' which remain on the trees after the leaves have fallen, well into the winter. Although sometimes seen as a tree, and a beautifully shaped one, too, the Hawthorn is usually planted as a hedge, for which purpose its spiny nature and its tolerance of clipping make it ideally suited. Another European species, also found in southern England, is the Midland Hawthorn (*Crataegus oxyacanthoides*), which is a smaller tree, oval leaved with hardly any lobing; but there is much hybridization

The cut, variable-shaped leaves and the round fruits of the Hawthorn.

Above
The creamy white flowers on the Hawthorn hedges herald the approach of summer in southern Britain.

Above right
The red-flowered cultivar of the Midland Hawthorn is often planted in gardens and on roadsides.

Right
The shiny red fruits of the Hawthorn provide a reserve food supply for the birds in late winter.

between the two species. It is chiefly because of the pretty, red-flowered cultivar, 'Paul's New Double Scarlet', so often seen in parks and gardens, that this species is mentioned here.

Most of the American thorn trees come from the eastern side of the country where there are several hundred species, the majority being very small trees or bushes. In general, they have bigger fruits than the European species and the leaves often colour beautifully in the autumn.

The Cockspur Thorn (*Crataegus crus-galli*), widely distributed from the St Lawrence River south through the Appalachians to North Carolina and east from Michigan to Illinois, grows to about 7·5 metres (25 feet) tall, has oval leaves entirely without lobes and slightly curved, sharply pointed spines some 100 millimetres (4 inches) long. Its bright-red berries are 13 millimetres ($\frac{1}{2}$ inch) in diameter and persist on the tree long after the orange autumn leaves have fallen. The Washington Thorn (*Crataegus phaenopyrum*) has a more southerly distribution from North Carolina, Tennessee, and Kentucky south to Mississippi, and is a 12-metre (40-foot) shapely tree with a thick crown of broadly lobed leaves very much like blackberry foliage in general shape, and changing to scarlet in the autumn. The fruits are a lustrous red persisting well into the winter. In the north-west the Black Hawthorn (*Crataegus douglasii*) ranges from British Columbia south through Washington and Oregon to California. Often just a shrub growing in thickets along mountain streams, it can be a tree up to 12 metres (40 feet) tall, with oval leaves, wedge shaped at the base; but the fruits are the distinct feature, being black and lustrous with a slight bloom and borne in drooping clusters. The Asiatic hawthorns are not nearly so numerous as the American. Two Chinese species which grow to 9 metres (30 feet) tall are *Crataegus pinnatifida* from the north of the country, which has large leaves 100 millimetres (4 inches) long with two big lobes either side of the base and spotted red fruit more than 13 millimetres ($\frac{1}{2}$ inch) in diameter, sweet and edible; and *Crataegus sanguinea*, with large, diamond-shaped leaves and bright-red, slightly smaller fruits. Both have white flowers 19 millimetres ($\frac{3}{4}$ inch) across – big for hawthorns. Strangely, there are no thorn trees native to Japan.

GENUS *Mespilus* medlars
(Latin name for Medlar)

A genus of one species of small, deciduous trees, closely related to the thorns and native to southern Europe.

The Medlar (*Mespilus germanica*) is a small, spiny, spreading tree up to 9 metres (30 feet) tall with oval leaves about 125 millimetres (5 inches) long which are crinkled, with sunken veins, and almost no stalk. The palest of pink flowers 38 millimetres ($1\frac{1}{2}$ inches) across, give rise to apple-shaped, brown, open-eyed fruits which are edible only when partially decayed, or better still when made into jelly.

The white fruits of another rowan, the Hupeh Rowan (*Sorbus hupehensis*), make it an attractive garden tree.

GENUS *Sorbus* whitebeams and rowans
(from *sorbum*, the Latin name for the fruit of the Service Tree)

A genus of about eighty species of small- to medium-sized, deciduous trees from all north temperate regions, Mexico, and the Himalayas, with simple or compound leaves, white flowers on clusters at the branch ends, turning into heads of berry-like fruits which are structually very like small apples.

The Rowan (*Sorbus aucuparia*), or Mountain Ash, is native to, and widely spread over, the cool temperate parts of Europe and western Asia, often at high altitudes where few other trees can survive. In sheltered situations, it can be as tall as 18 metres (60 feet) when its rounded crown of ascending branches, bearing 150-millimetre (6-inch) long, feathery leaves, composed of six-and-a-half or seven-and-a-half pairs of toothed leaflets astride a central stalk, make it a particularly attractive tree and doubly so in spring when masses of white flowers hang from the branch ends, and again in late summer before the red berries are eaten by Blackbirds and before, on exposed sites, the leaves turn red in the autumn. The True Service Tree (*Sorbus domestica*) is a very similar tree but rarer and native to southern Europe, North Africa,

Two Rowans, one in summer leaf and the other in typical autumn reds, add colours to a mountain scene.

Sorbus

151

and south-west Asia. The main difference is that it has green buds as opposed to purplish ones in the Rowan, and the fruits are green, tinged with reddish brown. The Wild Service Tree (*Sorbus torminalis*), however, with a wider distribution extending through all of Europe south of Denmark, including southern Britain, has Maple-like leaves with triangular lobes and brown fruit. It also has green buds.

The Whitebeam (*Sorbus aria*) a native of southern England and central and southern Europe, grows up to 15 metres (50 feet) tall and is, in spring, one of the most attractive of the genus. The oval, finely toothed leaves emerge, clothed all over in fine, white down, later becoming smooth and bright green above but retaining the down beneath, to flutter and glitter with silvery whiteness throughout the summer, before turning light brown in the autumn. The tree thrives only on chalky soils. The Swedish Whitebeam (*Sorbus intermedia*) is a tree of similar size from Sweden, the Baltic States, and north-east Germany. It tends to be more branched, with a shorter bole than the Whitebeam, and leaves with teeth at the tips becoming lobes towards the base. The tree is frequently planted in parks and streets, especially in Britain.

The American Mountain Ash (*Sorbus americana*), a native of eastern North America from Newfoundland to Virginia, is very like the European Rowan but has larger leaves, up to 0·3 metre (1 foot) long, and its winter buds are sticky, as opposed to hairy in the Rowan. Another very similar species, *Sorbus decora*, ranges further north into Labrador and has broader leaflets and larger, bright-orange fruits. This species is often planted in gardens in eastern parts of North America because of the beauty of its fruits.

The Himalayan Whitebeam (*Sorbus cuspidata*) is found in those mountains from Garwhal eastwards to Sikkim, and is a very handsome tree some 15 metres (50 feet) tall, chiefly remarkable for its very large leaves. Over 200 millimetres (8 inches) long, they are typical, oval, whitebeam leaves with cobweb-like down on the upper surfaces immediately after opening, which falls away later; but the white felt on the undersides persists. The white flowers, 19 millimetres ($\frac{3}{4}$ inch) across, give way to red, speckled, round, fruits of similar size. A hybrid between this species and the European Whitebeam, *Sorbus* 'Wilfred Fox', has slightly smaller but wider leaves and is sometimes planted in parks and gardens.

Vilmorin's Rowan (*Sorbus vilmorinii*) comes from western China and is a small tree about 9 metres (30 feet) tall with classic rowan compound leaves bearing eight-and-a-half to twelve-and-a-half pairs of leaflets. It is remarkable for its fruits, however, which, although red at first, become white, tinged with pink. The Chinese Whitebeam (*Sorbus folgneri*), a tree of the same size, is notable for its rather pointed, narrow leaves that are vividly white beneath, retaining this attribute even after the upper surfaces have turned brilliant red in the autumn, giving a spectacular display.

The Japanese Rowan (*Sorbus commixta*) is a very close relative of the American and European species and is found in the subalpine forests of that country as well as in Korea. Its leaves are bigger than the other species but the leaflets are greenish white on their undersides and the fruits remain an orange-red. But it is the autumn colouring of this tree which is remarkable; the whole crown becomes purple mixed with patches of scarlet and this species, together with another which turns brilliant scarlet, the Chinese Scarlet Rowan (*Sorbus discolor*), is becoming increasingly popular as a roadside and garden ornamental.

Another Japanese species, also found in China, Taiwan, and Korea, is *Sorbus alnifolia*, a tree about 13·5 metres (45 feet) tall which, as the name implies, has Alder-shaped, shiny leaves. The white flowers are 13 millimetres ($\frac{1}{2}$ inch) across and borne in rather sparse bunches. The fruits, which are scarlet without any calyx adhering, are spotted with black and look like ladybirds. The timber of the Japanese species is put to good use for furniture, turnery, and fuel.

GENUS *Malus* apples
(Latin name for apple)

A genus of some twenty-five species of medium-sized to small, deciduous trees from the north temperate parts of North America, Europe, and Asia. From these, an enormous number of hybrids and cultivars has

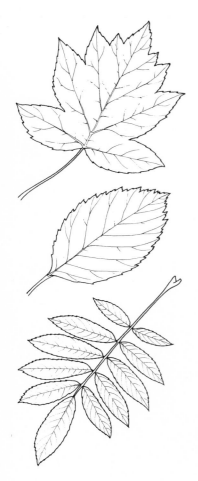

Top
Maple-like leaf of the Wild Service Tree.
Centre
Oval, toothed leaf of the Whitebeam.
Bottom
Compound leaf of the Rowan.

Left
In late spring the Whitebeam produces clusters of white flowers at the branch ends.

Below
The downy, white, unfolding leaves of the Whitebeam light up the whole tree in springtime.

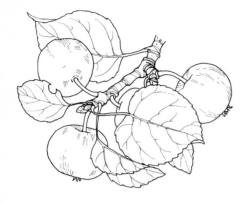
The oval leaves and the fruits of the Crab Apple.

arisen or has been raised both for fruit and for ornament. The leaves are usually oval with toothless margins, or very finely toothed, and the fruits are round or oval.

The Crab Apple (*Malus sylvestris*) is native to Europe and south-west Asia and is the tree from which all cultivated apples were originally derived. It grows to some 10·5 metres (35 feet) tall and has oval leaves. The flowers are a very faint pink and the round fruits, which are 25 millimetres (1 inch) in diameter, are green, turning yellow, tinged with red, when ripe.

Nine species of wild apples are native to North America, of which the Prairie Crab Apple (*Malus ioensis*), is one of the more widespread in the central states. It is about 9 metres (30 feet) tall with downy branches which persist in this condition all winter. It has oval leaves, 100 millimetres (4 inches) long. The rose-coloured flowers are very fragrant and the yellowish-green fruit is 38 millimetres (1½ inches) in diameter.

The Oregon Crab Apple (*Malus fusca*) is a rather bigger tree, up to 12 metres (40 feet) tall, and native to the north-west from the Aleutians south through British Columbia down the Pacific Coast to California, reaching its largest size in Washington and Oregon. The leaves are oval with abrupt, tapering points, turning bright orange and scarlet in the autumn. The pink flowers give way to little yellow apples, flushed with red and 19 millimetres (¾ inch) in diameter. In the east, from Ontario to New York, the Garland Crab Apple (*Malus coronaria*), which can grow to heights of 9 metres (30 feet) but is more often a multistemmed, broad-crowned tree in dense thickets, has beautiful big flowers, 50 millimetres (2 inches) across, that are pale pink and perfumed like violets. The fruits are yellowish green and very sour.

The Asiatic crab apples are remarkable for their floral beauty and none more so that the Japanese Crab Apple (*Malus floribunda*), a tree some 9 metres (30 feet) tall which, in April, on its low, domed crown produces, amid its deep-green leaves, an immense profusion of red flower buds which open pink and later turn white, giving way to little reddish apples on long stalks; while another Japanese species, the Pillar Apple (*Malus tschonoskii*), grows narrow and erect with white flowers and leathery leaves which turn a spectacular red in the autumn. The Hupeh Crab Apple (*Malus hupehensis*) from western China and the eastern Himalayas, is a tree with very stiff branches, level but ascending towards the tips to make a wineglass shape. The fragrant flowers are 19 millimetres (1½ inches) across and rose pink on opening. The fruit is small and yellow-green with patches of red.

GENUS *Pyrus* pears
(the Latin for a pear)

The fruits of the Wild Pear, although green at first, turn brown when ripe.

A genus of medium-sized to small deciduous trees from Europe, Asia Minor, north Africa, and north-east Asia, very like apples but with fruits tapering at the base and containing grit cells in the flesh.

The Common Pear (*Pyrus communis*), a native of Europe and western Asia, is the originator of all cultivated pears. It grows to over 15 metres (50 feet) in height, often cone shaped with bark which cracks into small squares distinguishing it from the apples. The flowers are white and appear before the leaves are fully open. The small pears are brown in colour.

Although the Gean produces a magnificent display of white flowers in the spring, the cherries are small, sour, and inedible.

Another European species is the more ornamental Willow-leaved Pear (*Pyrus salicifolia*) but it is rarely more than 9 metres (30 feet) tall. It has pendulous, downy branches with pale-grey, narrow leaves and pure white flowers 13 millimetres ($\frac{3}{4}$ inch) across; their stalks are also covered with white wool.

The Kumaon Pear (*Pyrus pashia*), from the central Himalayas, often reaches 10·5 metres (35 feet) in height and is distinct among pears in having its rose-tinted flowers closely packed in rounded clusters, the red stamens adding to the overall effect. The pears are nearly round but are not indented where the stalks join them, as in apples.

GENUS *Prunus* plums, almond, apricots, peaches, cherries
(the Latin name for cherry)

A genus of over 200 species of medium-sized to small, deciduous and evergreen trees from temperate regions of North America, Europe, and Asia, with five-petalled flowers and one-celled, one-seeded fruits.

The Gean (*Prunus avium*) is the common wild cherry of Europe, north Africa, and western Asia. It is a large and graceful tree with thin, scaly bark which peels horizontally, and a regularly shaped crown of oblong to oval leaves with red stalks, and red glands near the leaf bases. The white flowers are borne in clusters at intervals along the young shoots, turning into red cherries which are always eaten by birds before

Prunus

156

they are really ripe. Close grown, this tree can be 30 metres (100 feet) tall, but is more usually about 18 metres (60 feet). It often grows on the fringe of beechwoods, white in the spring and yellowish red in the autumn. The timber is even grained, yellowish brown and works well, taking a good polish. It is now in fashion again for furniture, although it is in fairly short supply.

The Bird Cherry (*Prunus padus*) is another European species extending into Asia Minor, and further north in Europe than the Gean. It is a smaller tree, often forking and rarely more than 15 metres (50 feet) tall with a drooping crown of leathery leaves with sunken veins, and little white flowers characteristically borne on hanging stalks about 150 millimetres (6 inches) long, producing a string of small, black, very sour cherries. The Cherry Plum (*Prunus cerasifera*), native to the Balkans and eastwards into central Asia, is a spreading small tree about 9 metres (30 feet) tall which opens its white flowers together with the leaves in early spring and is often mistaken for the Blackthorn. Two cultivars of this species 'Nigra' and 'Atropurpurea' are the copper-leaved cherries often seen in parks and gardens, the former with pink flowers and the latter with white.

Two species of evergreen cherries are native to Europe. The Portugal Laurel (*Prunus lusitanica*) comes from Spain and Portugal and can grow up to 15 metres (50 feet) tall. It has 75- to 125-millimetre (3- to 5-inch) long, glossy green, oval leaves with toothed margins and rather yellow beneath, and 250-millimetre (10-inch) long spikes of white flowers of which only a few develop into little black cherries with pointed tops. The Cherry Laurel (*Prunus laurocerasus*) is a smaller tree, barely 9 metres (30 feet) tall, but with bigger leaves, up to 200 millimetres (8 inches) long, and much shorter flower spikes, only 75 millimetres (3 inches) long but bearing bigger cherries nearly 25 millimetres (1 inch) in diameter. Both these species are usually planted as hedges in milder parts, often near the sea.

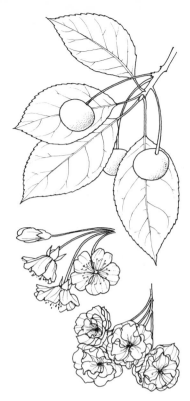

Top
Leaves and fruit of the Gean.
Centre
Flowers of the Gean.
Bottom
Flowers of the double-flowering variety of the Gean.

Left
The flowers of the Bird Cherry are borne on long, hanging shoots.

Above
The evergreen Cherry Laurel makes an excellent hedge where weather conditions are not severe.

157

The Almond (*Prunus dulcis*) has been in cultivation in southern Europe and western Asia for centuries and its original native home is not known for certain, but is probably in north Africa. The type tree is about 9 metres (30 feet) tall and has narrow, dark-green leaves partially wrapped round the twig at the base, and pink flowers borne on very short stalks which come out long before the leaves – one of the earliest blossoms in the spring. The fruits are green and hairy, drying up and splitting to reveal a stone with a pitted shell the kernel of which is the almond. Numerous varieties are cultivated for their fruit. The Peach (*Prunus persica*), another species so long in cultivation that its origin is in doubt, but is probably China, is closely related to the Almond. It bears pink flowers before the leaves. The fruit, too, is downy but is fleshy and sweet round the stone, like that of the Apricot (*Prunus armeniaca*), also from China, and a tree of the same size and shape as the peach, some 9 metres (30 feet) tall.

The largest of the American species is the Black Cherry (*Prunus serotina*), native to all the eastern states and south-east Canada from Nova Scotia to Minnesota and from Florida to Texas, with varieties in New Mexico and Mexico. It can be as tall as 30 metres (100 feet) in the southern Appalachians, with the main branches very upright but drooping towards the ends to form a broad somewhat spreading crown. The leaves are oval and shiny green above with incurved teeth on the margins. The white flowers are borne on 150-millimetre (6-inch), dropping clusters, like the Bird Cherry, and produce strings of pea-sized, black cherries popular only with birds. The timber is extensively used for veneers, furniture, and cabinet making. The American Wild Plum (*Prunus americana*) is a wide-spreading tree about 10·5 metres (35 feet) tall from the middle and northern states. It has oval, pointed leaves appearing at the same time as the pink to red flowers which produce 25-millimetre (1-inch) long, bright red plums without any bloom. The Canada Plum (*Prunus nigra*), with a much more northerly range into south-east Canada, bears a rather larger, orange-red fruit.

The pink blossoms of the Almond, which flowers before the leaves emerge, are some of the earliest to appear in the spring.

The Amanogawa Cherry grows narrow and upright, and is an ideal tree for small gardens.

Of the evergreen American species, the Islay (*Prunus ilicifolia*) is a small tree about 9 metres (30 feet) tall from the coastal ranges of California south of San Francisco. It has small, oval, thick, leathery leaves with spine-toothed margins, like Holly, and white flowers on short spikes which produce dark-purple cherries. The species from the east is the American Mock Orange (*Prunus caroliniana*), a 12-metre (40-foot) tree found mainly in coastal regions from North Carolina to Texas. It has 115-millimetre ($4\frac{1}{2}$-inch) long, pointed, leathery leaves, not unlike those of citrus fruits, and bears little black cherries on short spikes. Both these evergreen species are planted as ornamentals.

The commonest wild cherry in Japan is Sargent's Cherry (*Prunus sargentii*), a tree up to 21 metres (70 feet) tall, found throughout those islands. It has large leaves, 100 millimetres (4 inches) long with sharp points, and they are copper coloured when they emerge, but dark green when fully developed. The beautiful, 19-millimetre ($1\frac{1}{2}$-inch), pink flowers come out with the leaves and are borne in pairs on long stalks. The timber is highly prized for furniture and musical instruments. The Rose-bud Cherry (*Prunus subhirtella*) is a small, erect tree about 9 metres (30 feet) tall with oval, pointed leaves that appear before the pink flowers. The type tree is less often seen than the cultivar, 'Autumnalis', the Winter-flowering Cherry, which starts to open its fringed-petalled, pink flowers in October and continues to do so until early spring. A hybrid between this type tree and another large Japanese cherry, *Prunus speciosa*, is one of the most floriferous roadside trees in Britain, namely the Yoshino Cherry (*Prunus* x *yedoensis*) which in April, produces, before the leaves, masses of deeply notched, white flowers in a broad, flat crown. But the 'father' of most of our flowering cherries is the Japanese Cherry (*Prunus serrulata*) which, as a type tree, is rarely seen and its place of origin is in doubt, although it is probably China. The cultivars are legion: 'Amanogawa' is narrow like a Lombardy

159

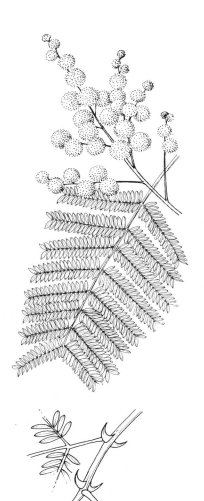

Top
The fluffy, yellow flower and the pale-grey, feathery leaves of the Silver Wattle.
Bottom
The strong, hooked thorns of the Apiesdoring.

Poplar with pale-pink flowers; 'Kanzan' is a broad tree with ascending branches carrying dense masses of deep-pink, double flowers; 'Shiro-fugen' with large, double, white flowers amid purplish, unfolding leaves on pendulous branches; and 'Tai-Haku', the largest-flowered cherry with blossoms 75 millimetres (3 inches wide).

The Tibetan Cherry (*Prunus serrula*), from Tibet and western China is a tree sometimes up to 15 metres (50 feet) tall with a broad crown and arched, upward-growing branches. The leaves are narrow and pointed. The little white flowers come out after the leaves have opened but are not significantly showy; it is the remarkable bark which marks this tree. It is a glossy brown, mahogany colour with pale-brown, horizontal bands, going right up into the branches where it peels in thin, translucent strips. Some grooming is necessary to keep the detached scales and sprouting shoots from spoiling the effect.

Family Leguminosae
GENUS *Acacia*
(from *akis*, a sharp point, referring to the spines)

A genus of about 400 species of thorny trees and shrubs, mainly evergreen, found in many tropical and subtropical regions, especially Australia and Africa. The leaves are usually feathery although sometimes they are apparently entire and simple, but in reality these are expanded leaf stalks or **phyllodes**. The flowers are usually yellow, borne in globular heads with just the stamens showing. The fruits are thin, pea-like pods, containing seeds.

The most valuable timber species in Australia is the Blackwood (*Acacia melanoxylon*) which is native to southern Queensland, New South Wales, Victoria, and Tasmania. It grows to 30 metres (100 feet) tall in the southern part of its range, especially in Tasmania, where it mixes with eucalyptus, often as an understorey. The leaves (phyllodes) are narrow, curved, and tapered to the base. The yellow flowers are carried thirty to fifty at a time on globular heads. The timber is golden brown, and in larger sizes, which are now rare, it is used for veneers. Most other Australian acacias are small trees that are important as ornamentals in many other countries. The Silver Wattle (*Acacia dealbata*), the Mimosa of southern Europe, is rarely more than 15 metres (50 feet) tall in its native south-east Australia. It has beautiful, feathery, pale-grey leaves and produces massed balls of fragrant yellow flowers. Perhaps even more beautiful is the Cootamundra Wattle (*Acacia baileyana*) from New South Wales which blossoms even more profusely and has a bluish tinge to its grey, feathery leaves.

The Australian wattles produce masses of fragrant, yellow flowers on globular heads, among delicate, feathery leaves.

The Ana Tree (*Acacia albida*) is one of the largest trees in northern south and central Africa, growing up to 27 metres (90 feet) tall in northern Transvaal and Rhodesia. It has grey bark and fine, feathery, blue-grey leaves. The smooth white twigs carry 25-millimetre (1-inch) long thorns in pairs and the creamy flowers are in spikes, not balls, giving way to very twisted, 100-millimetre (4-inch) long pods, relished by stock and game. A large tree will produce a tonne of pods in a year. The Apiesdoring (*Acacia galpinii*) can grow up to 24 metres (80 feet) tall and is a fine sight along the rivers of the Transvaal bushveld with its light-green, luxuriant, feathery foliage, and its whitish-yellow, flaky bark. The thorns, on the trunk and branches as well as the twigs, are short and strongly hooked like a hawk's beak. The Camel Thorn (*Acacia giraffae*), with its umbrella-like crown some 9 metres (30 feet) tall, is one of the most conspicuous trees in the drier, sandier parts of northern South Africa, Rhodesia, and south-west Africa. The twisting twigs are armed with powerful, sharp thorns and the fine foliage becomes very dense after the yellow balls of flowers have faded. The half-moon-shaped pods, 125 millimetres (5 inches) long and covered with grey felt, are readily eaten by stock and are the distinctive feature of this tree which is slow growing and very long lived. The Umbrella Thorn (*Acacia tortilis*) is found throughout the drier parts of Africa from the Orange Free State up to Arabia. In shape, it resembles an umbrella turned inside out by the wind, rarely reaching more than 9 metres (30 feet) tall. The small, 25-millimetre (1-inch) leaves are very finely feathered and the sulphur-yellow, sweet-scented flowers develop into curly, twisted pods, preferred above all others by cattle. The twigs

Below
Many of the African acacias are armed with long, sharp thorns. This specimen also bears parasitic galls.

Below right
Their yellow bark distinguishes these Fever Trees in the Kenya bush.

GENUS *Cladrastis*
(from *klados*, branch, *thruastos*, fragile)

A genus of four species of medium-sized, deciduous trees, from North and South America, and eastern Asia, the large, compound leaves with an uneven number of leaflets, alternate and not opposite on the midrib, pea flowers and buds hidden by the base of the leaf stalk.

The American Yellowwood (*Cladrastis lutea*) is a tree rarely more than 15 metres (50 feet) tall with a very limited distribution in Tennessee, Alabama, and Arkansas. It is broad and graceful with ascending branches bearing the 300-millimetre (12-inch) compound leaves and the wide, drooping clusters of white flowers, hanging from the twig ends on thin stalks, and turning into flat pods. The heartwood is bright yellow when first cut, yielding a yellow dye, darkening later to a brown streaked with yellow, when it is used for making gunstocks. The Japanese Yellowwood (*Cladrastis platycarpa*) is a similar-sized tree, found only in the south of that country and differing from the American species in having more pointed leaflets, each with a little **stipel** (stalklet) at the base of its stalk, and a wing round each seed pod. The Chinese Yellowwood (*Cladrastis chinensis*), like the Japanese species, carries its flowers on an upright stalk.

GENUS *Delonix*
(from *delos*, clear)

A genus of three medium-sized, tropical trees from Africa and Asia, with doubly compound, feathery leaves, very large flowers, and huge, long, woody pods.

The Flame of the Forest (*Delonix regia*), a native of Madagascar, is one of the most spectacular of tropical trees. Up to 18 metres (60 feet) tall, with an umbrella-shaped crown of 0·6-metre (2-foot) feathery leaves, it bears 125-millimetre (5-inch) wide scarlet flowers progressing up the tree from the axils of the earliest leaves and covering the whole tree in a fantastic display every six months or so. The flowers start opening during the night and are fully out from 9.00 a.m. onwards, lasting only two days. The tree is usually planted in avenues and along streets.

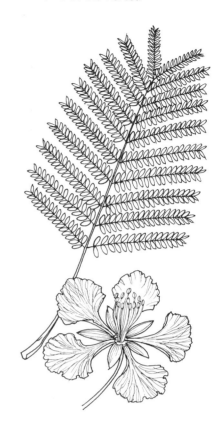

The feathery leaf and the big, scarlet flower of the Flame of the Forest.

The Flame of the Forest is one of the most spectacular of tropical flowering trees and is extensively planted as an ornamental.

The compound leaf with pointed leaflets of the Pagoda Tree.

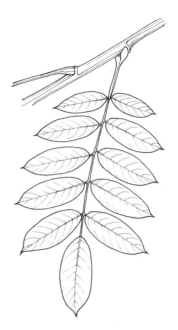

Above
The eastern North American Black Locust has become naturalized in central and southern Europe and is a mass of white flowers in May.

Above right
The contorted branches of the Pagoda Tree give it a venerable and majestic appearance.

GENUS *Sophora*
(from an Arabic name alluding to the butterfly shape of the flowers)

A genus of some twenty species of evergreen and deciduous trees and shrubs native to subtropical and warm temperate regions of North and South America, Australasia, and Asia, with double compound leaves, pea flowers on special stalks, and pods which are constricted between the seeds.

The Pagoda Tree (*Sophora japonica*) comes from China and Korea and is a rounded-crowned tree often with very twisted and contorted branches, and up to 24 metres (80 feet) tall. The 250-millimetre (10-inch) long, compound leaves have rather pointed leaflets, and the white flowers, borne on and around equally long stalks, do not appear until late summer, falling when still fresh and unfaded to make the ground beneath quite white. The Kowhai (*Sophora tetraptera*), a native of New Zealand, is a small, evergreen tree seldom more than 9 metres (30 feet) tall but, because of its beautiful feathery leaves, each with seventy leaflets, and its masses of golden blossom is generally considered as that country's national flower.

GENUS *Laburnum*
(Latin name for this tree)

A genus of three species of small, deciduous, flowering trees found in southern Europe and western Asia. The leaves have three leaflets and the pea-like flowers are borne on hanging stalks.

The Common Laburnum (*Laburnum anagyroides*) is native to central and southern Europe and is a small tree seldom more than 9 metres (30 feet) tall. With its long, pendulous strings of yellow flowers, it is one of the well-loved early summer sights in much of Europe, although this species is being superseded in many gardens and parks by Voss's Laburnum (*Laburnum* x *watereri*) a hybrid between it and the so-called Scotch Laburnum (*Laburnum alpinum*) which has longer and denser strings of flowers and a more leafy crown than the common species.

GENUS *Robinia* false acacias
(after Jean Robin, herbalist to Henry IV and Louis XIII of France)

A genus of twenty species of deciduous trees and shrubs from North America and Mexico, with compound leaves, pea-shaped flowers on long, pendulous stalks, and leaf stipules developed as spines.

The Black Locust (*Robinia pseudoacacia*) is a tree up to 24 metres (80 feet) tall found in the Appalachian Mountains from Pennsylvania to Georgia. It has a rounded crown of rather twisting, brittle branches and rugged, deeply furrowed bark on the bole. The leaves are up to 300 millimetres (12 inches) long with thirteen to fifteen leaflets and are usually yellowish green. The white flowers hang, laburnum-like, in dense sprays, in some years giving a magnificent display. The tree, introduced to Europe by Robin's son in the early 1600s, has become naturalized all over the Continent and in Britain, spreading by root suckers, especially on light, sandy soils. The timber is very hard and resistant to decay, making excellent fencing posts. A cultivar 'Frisia', has golden leaves and is a popular garden tree.

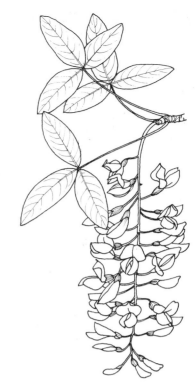

The trifoliate leaves and pendulous string of yellow flowers of the Laburnum.

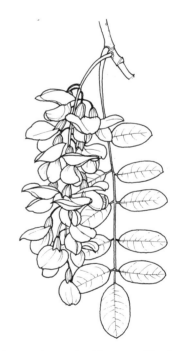

The dense spray of white, pea-like flowers and the compound leaf of the Black Locust.

The hanging tresses of yellow flowers are the Laburnum's worthy contribution to the early summer scene.

169

Above
Lemons have fairly smooth skins unlike Citrons, which are rough and knobbly.

Right
Orange blossom is white and fragrant, set amidst the shiny, thick, green leaves.

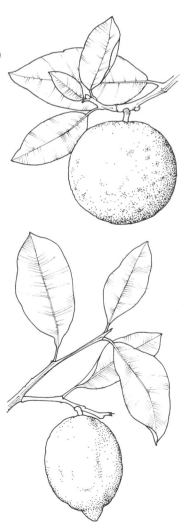

Top
The sweet orange developed originally from the Chinese species.
Bottom
The Lemon.

Family Rutaceae
GENUS *Citrus* oranges, lemons, grapefruits
(the Latin name for the Citron)

A genus of about thirty species of small, evergreen trees, from China and tropical Asia, which have all parts smelling of orange or lemon when crushed; thick, shiny, simple leaves; white, fragrant flowers; and pulpy, many-seeded fruits surrounded by a rind.

Although often mere bushes and only occasionally small trees, members of this genus and their varieties are so important economically and are planted so extensively in the warmer and sunnier parts of the globe, that mention of some of them must be made. The Citron (*Citrus medica*), originally from India and China, and introduced to Europe by Alexander the Great, produces rough-skinned fruits, used for making candied peel, and may be the species from which all oranges and lemons originated. The Lemon (*Citrus limon*) has a smoother-skinned fruit but it is very sour. Less sour is the Seville Orange (*Citrus aurantium*), used for making marmalade; the Sweet Oranges come from *Citrus sinensis*. Two species with skins which adhere to the inner part of the fruit are the Grapefruit (*Citrus paradisi*) and the Pumelo (*Citrus grandis*), the latter from Malaya with fruits often as much as 250 millimetres (10 inches) in diameter and not very juicy. The Lime (*Citrus aurantifolia*) has small, thin-skinned, green fruits and very acid pulp. Quite the opposite is the Tangerine (*Citrus reticulata*) with skin which comes away almost in one piece.

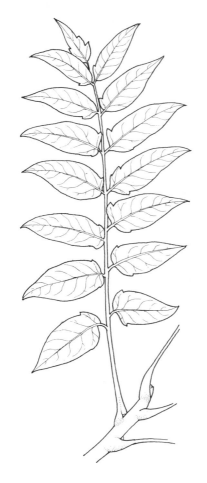

The large, thick-stalked leaf of the Tree of Heaven.

The broad crown of the Tree of Heaven bears big, thick-stalked, compound leaves and its tolerance of air pollution makes it popular for urban planting.

Family Simaroubaceae
GENUS *Ailanthus*
(a Latinized corruption of a Moluccan name meaning 'sky tree')

A genus of 150 mainly tropical trees from Asia, with large, compound leaves and insignificant flowers, but brightly coloured wings on the seeds.

The Tree of Heaven (*Ailanthus altissima*), from northern China, is a large, deciduous tree occasionally up to 27 metres (90 feet) tall with a stout bole and upright, thick branches supporting an open crown of big, thick-stalked leaves, 460 millimetres (18 inches) long with up to thirty narrow, pointed leaflets, each with one or two teeth and a small gland near the base. The flowers, male and female as a rule on separate trees, are borne in clusters on stalks at the ends of the branches, and the fruits are winged like those of Ash trees, becoming bright crimson and very decorative. The tree is very tolerant of pollution and is common in parks and squares in many large cities – usually female trees are grown because the male flowers smell objectionably.

Family Meliaceae
GENUS *Cedrela*
(from the Latin *cedrus*, cedar, because of the similarity of the wood)
A genus of sixty species of trees and shrubs, mainly from tropical Asia

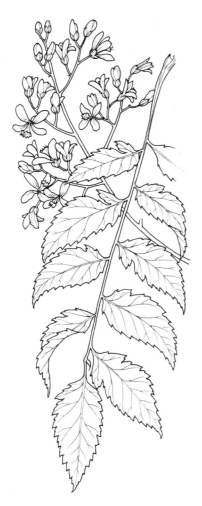

The purple flowers of the Pride of India give way to golden-brown berries.

The flower cluster and the toothed leaflets of the Pride of India.

and America, and including some valuable timber trees, which have compound leaves, flowers in bunches on stalks at the ends of the branches and fruit in the form of a woody capsule.

The West Indian Cedar (*Cedrela odorata*) is native to the West Indies, Mexico, and tropical South America. It grows to 30 metres (100 feet) tall on a trunk with a buttressed base and has 0·6-metre (2-feet) long compound leaves with eight pairs of widely spaced leaflets and none at the end of the stalk. The small flowers are yellow. The fragrant timber is used for fine furniture, panelling, and especially for cigar boxes. The Chinese Cedar (*Cedrela sinensis*) is a smaller tree about 21 metres (70 feet) tall and native to the north and west of that country. It has very large leaves, 0·75 metre (2½ feet) long with fifteen pairs and a terminal leaflet, although it rarely reaches its full size in China because its young branches are continually lopped and eaten as a vegetable. The flowers are white and the reddish timber is used for making furniture.

GENUS *Melia*
(from the Greek for the Ash tree, because of the similarity of the leaves)

A genus of twelve species of small- to medium-sized trees from the tropical Old World, with compound leaves, flowers bunched on stalks in the axils of the leaves and berry-like fruits.

The Pride of India (*Melia azedarach*), sometimes called Persian Lilac or the Bead Tree, is a native of northern India and is usually about 12 metres (40 feet) tall. The 460-millimetre (18-inch) long leaves are compound with six to eight toothed leaflets and an extra-long, pointed one at the end. The flowers, purple and fragrant, are clustered on stalks, developing into golden-brown berries eaten by birds but apparently poisonous to mammals – half a dozen can kill a man. Nevertheless, the tree, with its fine, feathery foliage and its pretty flowers and fruits, is much planted in parks and gardens in warm countries as an ornamental. The Indian Neem Tree (*Melia indica*) deserves mention because it is pervaded throughout with a strongly antiseptic resin making almost every part of it useful: its leaves pressed in books repel insects; its sap is distilled for medicinal toddy and soaps; and toothpaste and lotions have distillations of various parts of the tree incorporated in them.

GENUS *Swietenia* true mahoganies
(after Dr G van Swieten, a Dutch physician)

A genus of seven species of more or less evergreen trees native to tropical America. They have compound leaves without a terminal leaflet, flowers in clusters on a stalk rising from the bases of the leaf stalks, and the fruits are large, woody capsules splitting into five parts to release numerous winged seeds.

The Broad-leaved Mahogany (*Swietenia macrophylla*), a native of Honduras, is a large tree up to 45 metres (150 feet) tall and 6 metres (20 feet) in girth, often with a buttressed bole. The leaves are 0·6 metre (2 feet) long bearing five or six pairs of glossy green leaflets with yellowish midribs. The flowers on stalks shorter than the leaves are greenish yellow and the fruits are remarkable, barrel-shaped objects 150 milli-metres (6 inches) tall. The West Indian Mahogany (*Swietenia mahagoni*) is a smaller tree with all its parts proportionally smaller. Both species are components of climax rainforests and both produce the best and most famous cabinet wood in the world, the latter's being harder and denser, but the former's in greater supply. The Honduras species has been planted commercially in many warm parts of the world and is also planted as a street and shade tree in Malaysia and other tropical areas.

The mahoganies, trees of tropical rainforests, produce the most famous cabinet wood in the world.

Right
The thick, green branches of the
Candelabra Tree do not die down each
year like those of most euphorbias
but are added to annually giving the
tree this strange shape.

Far right
The Common Box is extremely
tolerant of clipping and can be trained
into fantastic shapes.

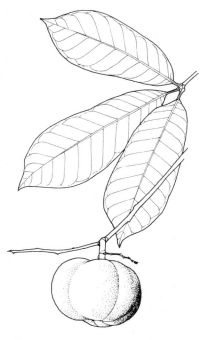

The trifoliate leaf and three-lobed fruit of
the Rubber Tree.

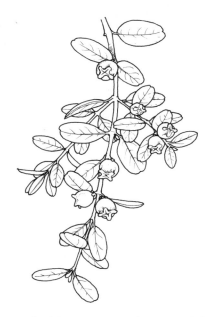

The small, shiny, evergreen leaves and the
female flowers of the Common Box.

Family Euphorbiaceae
GENUS *Euphorbia*
(from a Latin plant name)

A huge genus of cactus-like plants from most of the warm, dry regions
of the world, some of which are small trees with thick, green branches,
which function as leaves, and small, fleshy flowers.

The Candelabra Tree (*Euphorbia ingens*), found in the Transvaal,
Swaziland, and Rhodesia, is a small, compact tree some 9 metres (30
feet) tall. The lower, thick, green branches do not die down annually
like other members of the genus but are continually added to above, the
result being a wide, candelabra-shaped tree. The small, fleshy flowers are
red and the branches when wounded exude an acrid, poisonous latex.
These curious trees are sometimes planted along roadsides in Africa.

GENUS *Hevea*
(from *heve*, a West Indian name)

A genus of some fifteen evergreen or briefly deciduous trees from the
Amazon basin with three-lobed leaves, yellowish-white flowers on
short terminal stalks, male and female in the same cluster, and fruit in
the form of a three-lobed capsule with a rind and a bony shell.

The Rubber Tree (*Hevea brasiliensis*) is a tree of the tropical rainforests of the Amazon valley where it can be 30 metres (100 feet) tall.
The leaves are three-lobed on long, slender stalks. The bark is grey and
smooth and the small, whitish flowers produce a large, three-lobed
fruit, each lobe containing a large seed. It was some of these seeds
which, in 1876, were taken to Kew and there germinated, the resulting
seedlings being shipped to Singapore. From this original stock all the
rubber plantations in Malaya and Indonesia are derived. The tree
grows much better in the Far East than in Brazil, and a thin sliver of
bark can be cut off each day for years on end to produce up to 100 grams
(4 ounces) of latex daily from each tree.

Family Buxaceae
GENUS *Buxus* box trees
(Latin name for Box tree)

A genus of about thirty species of small, evergreen trees and bushes
from northern subtropical and temperate regions. The leaves are
small, round, and glossy, and set opposite one another on the twigs.
The petalless flowers are clustered at the bases of the leaves, one
female surrounded by about six males.

The Common Box (*Buxus sempervirens*), a native of Europe, northern
Africa, and western Asia, is often a shrub or planted as a hedge but can
be a tree 9 metres (30 feet) tall when it has a somewhat sinuous trunk
very often leaning to one side. The little, oval, shiny green leaves are
densely set on the twigs, with very short stalks. It is a tree of chalky
soils and its main use is in hedge form when it stands clipping well and is
easily kept neat and tidy.

Family Anacardiaceae
GENUS *Mangifera* mango trees

A genus of forty species of medium-sized, evergreen trees from India and south-east Asia with simple, upturned, leathery leaves, flowers on large terminal stalks, and large, fleshy, oblong fruit, usually with a flattened stone.

The Indian Mango (*Mangifera indica*), a spreading tree sometimes up to 24 metres (80 feet) tall, but usually smaller in cultivation, and in the countless varieties which have been developed, is native to India and probably Malaya. It has narrow, pointed leaves up to 300 millimetres (12 inches) long and whitish fragrant flowers on stalks nearly 0.6 metre (2 feet) long, bearing the smooth-skinned, orange-coloured fruits which are oblong and very variable in size, sometimes 150 millimetres (6 inches) long, usually less and often sweeter when they are smaller. The outer rind covers an orange flesh which has a sweet, albeit somewhat turpentine-tainted, flavour and surrounds a single, flattened, fibre-covered stone. Mangos are grown in orchards in many different varieties.

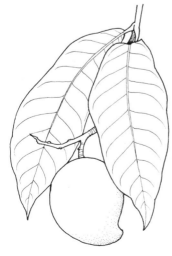

The pointed, evergreen leaves and the oblong, fleshy fruit of the Mango.

The large, compound leaves and the felt-covered twig of the Stag's Horn Sumach.

GENUS *Rhus*

A genus of over 100 species of small, evergreen and deciduous trees and shrubs found in most subtropical and temperate regions. They usually have compound leaves and flowers in clusters at the ends of the shoots. The fruits are small berries.

The Stag's Horn Sumach (*Rhus typhina*) ranges from New Brunswick along the St Lawrence valley to Ontario and south along the Appalachians and down the Atlantic seaboard. It can reach 12 metres (40 feet) in height and has 0·6-metre (2-foot) long, thick-stalked, compound leaves with eleven to thirty-one pointed, narrow leaflets which turn orange, scarlet, and purple in the autumn. The brownish flowers are closely packed in cone-shaped clusters at the ends of the branches. But the most striking thing about this tree is the covering of brown felt on the branches and twigs, resembling the antlers of a stag in velvet.

The Varnish Tree (*Rhus verniciflua*) comes from China, Japan, and the Himalayas where it can be as tall as 30 metres (100 feet) and a fine deciduous tree bearing big, compound leaves over 0·75 metre (2½ feet) long with up to nineteen narrow, pointed leaflets. They colour a beautiful red in the autumn. This tree is the source of Japanese lacquer which oozes out as a white, syrupy fluid from incisions in the bark.

Family Aquifoliaceae
GENUS *Ilex* hollies
(the Latin name for the Evergreen Oak which has similar leaves to the hollies)

A genus of about 300 species of evergreen and deciduous trees and shrubs, found throughout the world with the exception of western North America and Australasia. Some have evergreen, prickly leaves, usually with male and female flowers on separate trees, the latter producing red or black berries.

The Common Holly (*Ilex aquifolium*) is native to all Europe except the far north, and the Mediterranean region. It can be a large tree, as tall as 24 metres (80 feet), with grey bark on a relatively slim bole, but it is more often a small tree or even a bush. The tough, shiny, dark-green leaves vary greatly; those on the lower part of the tree have spines all round the margins and the higher up the tree the fewer the spines until at the top the leaves are smooth margined. The white flowers are clustered in the axils of the leaves, those on the female trees yielding the well-known red berries so much in demand at Christmas and eaten by the birds in February. There are many cultivars of this species including those with silver and gold leaf margins and those with tight and upright habits.

Below left
The Stag's Horn Sumach has velvet-covered branches and the leaves turn orange and scarlet in the autumn.

Below
Female Holly trees bearing the berries so much prized for Christmas decorations.

The Sycamore can reach a great size even on an exposed site.

The American Holly (*Ilex opaca*) is found only in the east and south of that country from Massachusetts to Florida and west into the Gulf states. It is a very similar tree to the Common Holly in nearly all respects except that the leaves are not so shiny and the flowers tend to be single or in pairs so that the fruit is less bunched and conspicuous. The timber, too, is of economic importance – it is hard, heavy, tough, and light in colour and it is used for cabinet work, turnery, musical instruments, and carving.

The Himalayan Holly (*Ilex dipyrena*), from eastern Nepal, Sikkim, and Bhutan, is a small tree about 12 metres (40 feet) tall with long, narrow leaves and the red berries well spaced out along the twigs. Two Japanese species are not at all Holly-like: *Ilex integra*, also found in South Korea, has lustrous leaves, but it is entirely without spines, and is common in coastal areas of southern Japan where its large, red berries make it a prized ornamental; and *Ilex macropoda* which has beautiful pale-green, yellow-veined deciduous leaves, sometimes eaten as vegetables, and bright-red, shiny berries. Both species grow to 13·5 metres (45 feet) tall and the white timber is used for turnery and marketry.

Family Aceraceae
GENUS *Acer* maples
(Latin name for maple which also means sharp because the wood was once used for spears)

A genus of over 200 species of large- to medium-sized deciduous trees from North America, Europe, and north-east Asia, with opposite, usually lobed leaves and fruits set opposite one another each with a wing attached.

The Sycamore (*Acer pseudoplatanus*) is Europe's largest maple and native to central and southern parts of the continent, but not to Britain

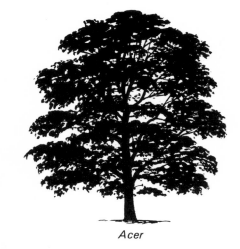

Acer

178

where it was introduced in Roman times. Open grown it is a fine, spreading tree 30 metres (100 feet) tall with a domed crown of five-lobed leaves 175 millimetres (7 inches) across, dark green above with blue-green undersides. The yellow flowers hang on a long stalk, the females at the top producing the familiar 'keys' which remain suspended long after the leaves have fallen, when the green buds are particularly noticeable. The white timber has many uses, and that with a wavy grain, produced by some trees, is particularly valuable for veneers. The other large European species is the Norway Maple (*Acer platanoides*), found in most of the continent south of southern Norway and Sweden excluding Britain, where it is an introduced tree. It, too, can grow up to 30 metres (100 feet) tall and has pale-grey, smooth bole, as opposed to the Sycamore's pinkish-brown, scaly bark. The leaves, too, differ in being a softer, paler green and thinner with sharp tips to the five lobes. They turn a beautiful yellow in the autumn. The wings of the 'keys' are more widely set than the Sycamore's.

A much smaller tree, often only a hedge plant but occasionally up to 18 metres (60 feet) tall, is the Field Maple (*Acer campestre*), native to all Europe, including Britain, western Asia, and north Africa. The older twigs have corky wings and the leaves are only 100 millimetres (4 inches) across cut deeply by the five lobes. The keys have the wings set at right angles. The Italian Maple (*Acer opalus*), from central and southern Europe, also rarely exceeds 18 metres (60 feet). It is a broad-domed, spreading tree with rather blunt-lobed leaves. The flowers are a feature; they are large and yellow and hang in dense bunches each on a long stalk. The keys have wings almost parallel to one another.

The Sugar Maple (*Acer saccharum*) is perhaps the best known of American maples. It ranges from south-east Canada down into the southern Appalachians and can exceed 30 metres (100 feet) in height with a rounded crown of leaves very similar to those of the Norway

The five-lobed leaf and seed 'key' of the Sycamore.

Left
The brilliant reds and yellows of the Sugar Maples are a feature of the north-east American landscape in the fall.

Above
The classic shape of the Norway Maple's yellowing autumn leaves.

179

The silvery undersides of the Silver Maple leaves catch the summer sun.

The Box Elder has a compound leaf with three to five leaflets.

Maple. These leaves turn brilliant reds and yellows in the autumn, and the tree is an outstanding feature of the northern landscape at that time of year. A single tree will produce up to 90 litres (20 gallons) of sugary sap each spring which, when boiled down, yields about 2·3 litres ($\frac{1}{2}$ gallon) of syrup. The timber is one of the most valuable of American hardwoods and is used for furniture and veneers, especially the accidental form with a curious grain called Bird's-eye Maple. Despite its confusingly similar name, the Silver Maple (*Acer saccharinum*) is a very different tree with nearly the same range but reaching further south and not so far north. It is a large, spreading tree, branching low down, the upright-growing branches weeping at their extremities and carrying the deeply indented, five-lobed leaves which are a shiny pale green above, silver white beneath, and small enough to flutter and flash in the sunlight. The keys, with almost parallel wings, fall in late summer and germinate immediately. The timber is soft and brittle and is used for cheap furniture and fuel.

An unconventional species is the Box Elder (*Acer negundo*) which has leaves with three to five leaflets, like those of the Ash. It is native to the whole of the eastern part of the country from New Brunswick to Ontario and from Florida to Texas, and is sometimes 21 metres (70 feet) tall but more usually about 15 metres (50 feet). It has a broad, bushy crown of compound leaves which turn yellow in the autumn, and male and female flowers are borne on separate trees, the latter producing v-shaped keys hanging on long stalks.

The Big-leaved Maple (*Acer macrophyllum*) is the only important species of the genus growing in the west of the country. It ranges from Alaska south through British Columbia down the coast and the coastal ranges to southern California, reaching its maximum development on alluvial soils in western Oregon where, close grown, it can be 30 metres (100 feet) tall or open grown have a crown spread of more than 18 metres (60 feet). The leaves are 300 millimetres (12 inches) across on 25-millimetre (1-inch) stalks and cut with three lobes half way to the midrib, with two other shallower lobes at the base. They turn a bright orange in the autumn, contrasting beautifully with the dark-green Douglas Firs which they so frequently attend in their natural range.

Two small Japanese maples and their cultivars have become very popular garden trees throughout the temperate world. The type tree in the case of the Smooth Japanese Maple (*Acer palmatum*) also found in China and Korea, is about 13·5 metres (45 feet) tall and common in the Japanese mountains. Its leaves have five to seven pointed, deep-cut lobes with toothed margins, borne on a network of thin, smooth branches in a bushy crown. This tree and its cultivars provide a wealth of autumn colour tints, the most brilliantly scarlet being 'Osakazuki'. The Downy Japanese Maple (*Acer japonicum*), only found in that country, is a similar-sized tree with leaves circular in outline, but cut into about ten shallow but pointed lobes, emerging covered in down which falls off later except from the lower veins. This tree, too, adopts autumnal tints of gold and scarlet, and a cultivar, 'Laciniatum', has

The 'Osakazuki' cultivar of the Japanese Smooth Maple is one of the reddest trees in the autumn.

The heavily cut leaf of the Japanese Maple and a hanging bunch of keys.

181

leaves with lobes cut almost to the midrib, these lobes themselves being cut into irregular teeth. The timber of both type trees is fine grained and is used for turnery, toys, and musical instruments.

A number of the Asiatic maples have very attractive bark. Hers's Maple (*Acer hersii*), a small tree about 9 metres (30 feet) tall and native to Hunan Province in China, is one which has smooth, olive-green bark striped with white in vertical lines giving it and others like it the general name of 'snake-bark' maples. The leaves are heart shaped at the base and broadly oval with three separate tips. They turn butter yellow in the autumn. But the Paper-bark Maple (*Acer griseum*), from western China, puts on an entirely different show. The bark is a dark, coppery brown, peeling in horizontal strips from the trunk and branches to reveal dark-red, smooth areas. The leaves are small with three leaflets, dark green and hairy above, blue-green and even more hairy beneath, turning deep red in the autumn and a fine sight above the chocolate bole.

Aesculus

Below right
The Horse Chestnut is one of the largest and most magnificent of all flowering trees.

Far right top
The spiky, green fruits of the Horse Chestnut contain the shiny, copper-red conkers.

Far right bottom
The flowers of the Red Horse Chestnut are attractive but the tree lacks the fine leaves and the noble habit of the common species.

Family Hippocastanaceae
GENUS *Aesculus* horse chestnuts, buckeyes
(Latin name for a kind of oak but used by Linnaeus to name this genus)

A genus of about twenty-five large- to medium-sized, deciduous trees, from North America, Europe, the Himalayas, China, and Japan with large, compound leaves, the leaflets spread out like the fingers of a hand, and flowers grouped on an erect stalk.

The Horse Chestnut (*Aesculus hippocastanum*), a native of a very restricted area in Albania and Greece, is one of the most magnificent flowering trees in the world but so common that its true merit is not always appreciated. Open grown, it forms a huge, symmetrical, domed crown often as much as 30 metres (100 feet) tall. The large, red-pointed buds become sticky in the spring and bring forth the 380-millimetre (15-inch) wide leaves of five to seven large, heavily veined leaflets arranged palm-fashion at the end of a stout stalk, to be quickly followed by pyramidal clusters of white flowers on 300-millimetre (12-inch) long, erect stalks. The effects of hundreds of these white 'candles' evenly spaced throughout the massive green crown is one of the most arresting of springtime sights. The fruits, which follow in the late summer, are round, spiny green husks containing one or two copper-red, shiny round nuts or 'conkers'. The Horse Chestnut is naturalized in many countries, including the whole of the eastern side of North America.

The largest of the American species is the Yellow Buckeye (*Aesculus octandra*) native to Pennsylvania and south to Ohio, Illinois, and Kentucky, where it can be over 24 metres (80 feet) tall. The leaves, borne on somewhat pendulous branches, are similar to those of the Horse Chestnut but half the size and downy on the undersides. The flowers, on 150-millimetre (6-inch) stalks, are yellow and the fruits are smooth without spines. The Ohio Buckeye (*Aesculus glabra*), a slightly smaller tree ranging a little further west, also has yellow flowers, but the leaflets are narrower and pointed and the fruit prickly, like the Horse Chestnut.

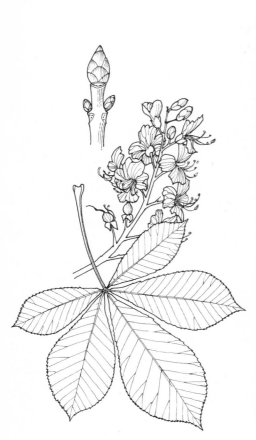

The large, pointed bud, the erect cluster of flowers, and the big, palmate leaf of the Horse Chestnut.

184

The Indian Horse Chestnut (*Aesculus indica*) is native to the north-west Himalayas from the Indus to Nepal where it is an even bigger tree than its European relative, sometimes as tall as 45 metres (150 feet). The leaves have slender, pointed, stalked leaflets, on a red main stalk, and the flowers are yellow flushed with red giving an overall pink colour. The fruits are rough but not spiny. It is much less often seen in cultivation than the Red Horse Chestnut (*Aesculus* x *carnea*), a hybrid between the Horse Chestnut and the shrubby American Red Buckeye (*Aesculus pavia*) which, despite its pretty flowers, lacks the fine leaves and the noble habit of the Indian species.

The Japanese Horse Chestnut (*Aesculus turbinata*), from central and southern parts of that country, and a tree often more than 27 metres (90 feet) tall, has immense leaves, over 0·6 metre (2 feet) in diameter which turn a brilliant orange in the autumn; but the flowers are smaller and less impressive than the European species. The fruit husks are warty but without spines. The tree is a popular ornamental in Japan and the flowers produce great quantities of honey.

185

Family Sapindaceae
GENUS *Nephelium*
(Greek for 'little cloud')

A genus of about seventy species of small, evergreen trees from tropical Asia and Australia, with compound, shiny, leathery leaves, small, yellowish-white flowers on terminal stalks, and large, hairy or knobbly fruits containing a single stone surrounded by white pulp.

The Lychee (*Nephelium litchi*) is a native of China but is extensively planted in many tropical countries for its fruit. It grows to about 15 metres (50 feet) tall with a broad, rounded crown of dark leaves, each with three to seven narrow, leathery leaflets casting a very deep and often welcome shade. The oblong fruits which succeed the flowers on 300-millimetre (12-inch) stalks, are 50 millimetres (2 inches) long, and have a brown, warty skin, flushed with red, containing a polished brown seed surrounded by a deliciously sweet, whitish, translucent flesh which tastes and 'feels' like grapes.

Family Tiliaceae
GENUS *Tilia* limes
(Latin name for the Linden tree)

A genus of about thirty species of large, deciduous trees ranging throughout the temperate regions of the Northern Hemisphere, except north-west America, with oval leaves that are heart shaped and often uneven at the base, and fragrant, honey-filled flowers on long stalks to which is attached for half its length, a single, membranous wing.

The Large-leaved Lime (*Tilia platyphyllos*) comes from continental Europe south from France to Spain and east to the Crimea. It is a large, narrow-domed tree up to 30 metres (100 feet) tall with roundish, heart-shaped rather hairy leaves with short, tapering points, about 125 millimetres (5 inches) long. The yellow flowers hang in threes and fours on 100-millimetre (4-inch), winged stalks attracting a great murmuration of bees in sunny June weather. The Small-leaved Lime (*Tilia cordata*) is a more northerly species, extending into Britain and Norway, and it is a rather smaller tree. The leaves are smaller and rounder than the large-leaved species and are bluish green on the undersides. The flowers do not open until late July. The Common Lime (*Tilia* x *europaea*) is a hybrid between the large- and small-leaved species and more commonly planted than either, despite its unfortunate habit of producing a profusion of shoots and sprouts round the bole,

Left
The Small-leaved Lime is a hardy tree which can reach a considerable size and might serve as a replacement for the dying elms in England.

Above
The fragrant, honey-filled flowers of the Lime hang on long, winged stalks.

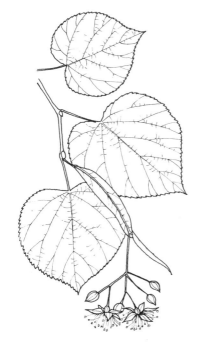

The heart-shaped leaves and the long-stalked flower of the Small-leaved Lime.

187

and often higher up on the larger branches. It grows taller than either of its parents, up to 36 metres (120 feet), but always looks untidy. The Silver Lime (*Tilia tomentosa*) is a native of south-eastern Europe and south-west Asia and has lop-sided leaves which are covered with dense grey down on their undersides making a fine show as they flutter in the summer breezes; and very like it is the Silver Pendant Lime (*Tilia petiolaris*), but its leaves are narrower and the leaf stalks longer giving a weeping effect.

The American Basswood (*Tilia americana*) is native to south-east Canada and the east and central United States from New Brunswick to Manitoba and from Oklahoma to North Carolina. It is a narrow-crowned tree up to 30 metres (100 feet) tall with broad, heart-shaped leaves some 8 inches long. The flowers are white giving way to pea-sized fruits, like all the limes. The White Basswood (*Tilia heterophylla*), with a much smaller range in the Carolinas and Georgia, has similar-sized leaves but with the undersides covered in silvery hairs.

The Japanese Lime (*Tilia japonica*) differs little from the Small-leaved Lime of Europe and is well distributed in the temperate forests of Japan and also in China. It is often planted as an ornamental and to attract bees, Like all other limes, it has a very tough underbark which is made into ropes.

GENUS *Hoheria*
(Latinized version of the Maori word *houhere*)

A genus of five species of medium-sized, evergreen trees native to New Zealand with shiny, dark-green leaves that are much paler on the undersides and with toothed margins, and white flowers in dense clusters in the axils of the leaves.

The Ribbonwood (*Honeria populnea*) is common throughout both islands, sometimes as much as 13·5 metres (45 feet) tall but more often a smaller shelter or hedge tree. With its shiny, Holly-like leaves and the beautiful white clusters of flowers, it is a pretty sight. The inner bark can be peeled in narrow strips and, being curiously perforated, looks like and was used as a substitute for lace.

The leaves of the Silver Pendant Lime have grey down on their undersides giving the tree a silvery green look.

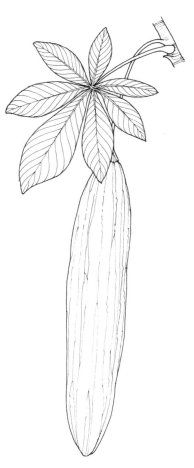

The palmate leaf and the woody fruit of the Baobab.

Family Bombacaceae
GENUS *Adansonia* baobabs
(after M Adanson, a French botanist)

The swollen, bottle-shaped trunk of the Baobab and its thick, spreading branches, resembling roots, have earned it the name of 'Upside-down Tree'.

A genus of large, evergreen or nearly deciduous trees native to Africa and Australia, with monstrous, swollen trunks, large, tortuous branches, sparse, compound leaves and large, single flowers developing into big, oblong, woody fruits.

The Baobab (*Adansonia digitata*) ranges from the Sudan to the Transvaal, and from the Cape Verde Islands east to Abyssinia. It is a tree of the dry savannas. The maximum height of this tree is about 23 metres (75 feet) but the enormous grossly swollen trunk is truly extraordinary. Cylindrical in shape, and more than 18 metres (60 feet) in diameter, the trunk suddenly tapers like a bottle and gives forth a spread of comparatively small branches resembling roots and accounting for the native name of 'Upside-down Tree'. From these branches sprout the twigs and palm-shaped leaves with stalkless, pointed leaflets, and from their axils hang the 150-millimetre (6-inch) wide, white flowers on 500-millimetre (20-inch) long stalks. The oblong 200-millimetre (8-inch) long fruits are covered in green 'velvet' enclosing a woody shell in which the black seeds are embedded in a white pulp relished by baboons. The huge trunk is valueless as timber, being designed for water storage. It is estimated that some of the largest trees contain up to 136 kilolitres (30 000 gallons) of water.

The Bottle Tree (*Adansonia gregori*), the Australian species, is a slightly smaller tree, but it is the same remarkable shape.

The fleshy red flower and the bursting seed capsule of the Silk-cotton Tree.

GENUS *Bombax*

A genus of eleven species of large, deciduous trees native to Africa India, Burma, Sri Lanka, and Malaysia with buttressed, spiny trunks and branches, compound, palm-shaped leaves, and single flowers developing into pods containing seeds embedded in silky fibres.

The Red Silk-cotton Tree (*Bombax malabaricum*), native to southern India and Sri Lanka, is a tall tree up to 45 metres (150 feet) in height, which is remarkable for the masses of large, fleshy, red flowers which cover its crown at the ends of the grey, spiny branches in January, before the leaves appear. The silky fibre from the seed pods is used in the same way as kapok, a substance obtained from trees of the genus *Ceiba*, a group of large trees found in tropical America and differing from *Bombax* in very minor ways.

GENUS *Ceiba*

The Kapok Tree (*Ceiba pentandra*) is a huge tree, bearing 230-millimetre (9-inch) long pods which burst to release the white floss which has so many commercial uses. The tree is extensively cultivated in tropical Asia for this product.

GENUS *Durio*
(from the Malay name, *durian*)

A genus of twelve species of large, nearly evergreen trees native to tropical Asia, with simple, pointed leaves, flowers in clusters attached directly to the trunk and branches, and large, thorny fruits containing pulp and seeds.

The Durian (*Durio zibethinus*) is a tree up to 30 metres (100 feet) tall widely cultivated in Malaya and elsewhere in the East for its fruits. In Malaya, every village has its Durian trees, tall and sombre with brownish leaves, and no-one who has lived there can forget (or describe) the strange, sickly-sweet smell which pervades the countryside when the football-sized, spiny fruits start to fall. The yellow, custardy pulp, relished by man, bird, and beast alike, tastes like strawberries and cream mixed with onions and is, oddly enough, a quickly acquired taste and lastingly relished.

GENUS *Ochroma*

A genus of a single species of medium-sized, evergreen trees, native to tropical South America with buttressed trunks, large, simple leaves, and bell-shaped flowers.

The Balsa Wood (*Ochroma pyramidale*) is a fast-growing tree up to 21 metres (70 feet) tall with extremely light wood, weighing only about 96 kilograms per cubic metre (6 pounds per cubic foot) when dry from trees specially quick grown for this purpose. Such trees can reach 12 metres (40 feet) in 18 months with girths of 0·6 metre (2 feet) and boles branch-free for 4·8 metres (16 feet). The wood is used in aircraft and for insulation. It was from these trees that the *Kon-Tiki* was made.

Family Sterculiaceae
GENUS *Theobroma*

A genus of about thirty species of small, evergreen trees, native to tropical South and Central America, with large, simple, leathery leaves and flowers borne directly on the trunk producing large, elliptical fruits.

The Chocolate Tree (*Theobroma cacao*) is a tree about 12 metres (40 feet) tall in the wild state, with 300-millimetre (12-inch) long, drooping, leathery leaves. The small, pink flowers appear on small bumps on the trunk and develop into ribbed, pointed fruits 300 millimetres (12 inches) long, red at first becoming green. These contain the seeds which, when roasted and pulverized, are made into cocoa after the fat has been removed, or chocolate if the fat is retained. Although the Aztecs domesticated the tree centuries ago, it is only since about 1850 that chocolate has become a world-wide confection. The tree is now planted extensively in many countries, especially west Africa.

Family Theaceae
GENUS *Camellia*

A genus of about eighty species of evergreen trees and shrubs native to India, China, and Japan, with small, simple leathery leaves and solitary flowers. The fruits are woody capsules containing several seeds.

The Common Camellia (*Camellia japonica*) is a small tree, 10·5 to 12 metres (35 to 40 feet) tall, common in the warm, temperate regions of southern Japan. It has smooth, shiny, simple leaves with serrated edges and beautiful red flowers 100 millimetres (4 inches) across with bunches of yellow stamens in the centre. The oil from the seeds is used for cooking and as hair oil in Japan.

Wild grown in its native monsoon forests of eastern India and western China, the Tea Plant (*Camellia thea*), is a small tree some 9 metres (30 feet) tall with short-stalked, shiny, oval leaves 100 millimetres (4 inches) long, and white, fragrant flowers 38 millimetres ($1\frac{1}{2}$ inches) across, borne in the leaf axils. When cultivated in tea gardens, it is kept as a low bush from which several times a year the new growth leaves are plucked. To make 0·45 kilogram (1 pound) of best-quality, manufactured tea, over 3000 branch tips must be picked, each usually a bud and two leaves.

GENUS *Stewartia*
(after John Stuart, 3rd Earl of Bute, a keen patron of horticulture)

A genus of ten species of small, deciduous trees and shrubs, native to eastern North America and eastern Asia, with smooth, tea-coloured bark, simple, oval leaves, and handsome white flowers.

The largest of the species is *Stewartia monadelpha*, a native of Japan and a tree up to 23 metres (75 feet) tall, common in the beech forests in the south of the country. The bark is smooth and a shiny, reddish brown colour and the pointed buds, especially on the vigorous shoots, often have subsidiary ones attached to them. The oval, yellowy green leaves are somewhat crinkled, and the 38-millimetre ($1\frac{1}{2}$-inch) wide white flowers have yellow stamens in the centre. Another Japanese species, *Stewartia pseudocamellia*, also has the attractive, orange-brown bark, and white-cupped flowers about twice the size. The leaves take on fine yellows and reds in the autumn.

Far left
Tea Trees are cultivated as bushes in tea gardens beneath the light shade of other trees.

Above
The white, waxy flower of the Tea Tree shows its close relationship to the camellias.

Below left
As well as bearing white, cupped flowers, the Japanese *Stewartia* has attractive orange-brown bark.

The shiny, oval leaves of the Tea Plant.

The large, white flower and the yellow-green leaves of the Japanese *Stewartia monadelpha*.

Right
Leaf sprays of the New Zealand
Pittosporum are often used in flower
arrangements.

Far right
The Black Tupelo is yet another
eastern North American tree which
turns glorious colours in the
fall.

Family Pittosporaceae
GENUS *Pittosporum*
(from *pitta*, pitch, and *sporum*, seed)

A genus of about 150 species of small, evergreen trees and shrubs, native for the most part to New Zealand and Australia, with simple, leathery, smooth-margined leaves and often fragrant flowers borne in the leaf axils.

The Tarata (*Pittosporum eugenioides*) or Lemonwood, is found throughout the lowland areas of New Zealand where it grows to a height of some 12 metres (40 feet) and is conspicuous in the 'bush' by virtue of the yellow-green colour of its elliptical leaves in contrast with the normal dark greens of the other trees. The attractive, yellow flowers are borne in honey-scented bunches and the fruits are oblong, woody capsules containing seeds embedded in a sticky secretion. The Karo (*Pittosporum crassifolium*) is a smaller tree seldom more than 9 metres (30 feet) tall, and largely a coastal species. The leaves are much thicker than the Tarata's and the flowers are chocolate coloured. It is planted for shelter on seaside sites because it is tolerant to wind and salt spray. A third species, *Pittosporum tenuifolium*, also a native of New Zealand, with wavy, crinkled, pale-green leaves on almost black twigs, is sometimes seen as a small bushy tree in gardens in southern England. The leaf sprays are often on sale in florists' shops in Britain.

The wavy, crinkled leaves of the
Pittosporum tenuifolium.

Family Nyssaceae

GENUS *Nyssa*
(from *nysa*, a water nymph)

A genus of six species of large, deciduous trees, native to eastern North America and eastern Asia, with single leaves, inconspicuous male and female flowers on separate heads, and small, berry-like fruits.

The Black Tupelo (*Nyssa sylvatica*) has a natural range from Maine to Florida and from Michigan to Texas, reaching its maximum height of 36 metres (120 feet) in the southern Appalachians of North Carolina and Tennessee. The horizontal branches and the glossy green, oval leaves, with smooth margins, form a dense, well-rounded crown. The little, greenish flowers appear with the leaves in heads on short stalks and develop into small, blue-black, plum-like fruits. The leaves turn a deep red in the autumn. Another species, the Water Tupelo (*Nyssa aquatica*), grows in swampy areas all along the eastern and Gulf coasts from Virginia to Texas and up the Mississippi valley to Illinois, and is only happy if it stands in water up to 0·9 metre (3 feet) deep for most of the year. It has oval but pointed leaves and the blue-black 'plums' are pear shaped. The tough timber of the tupelos is used for furniture, crating, and boxes.

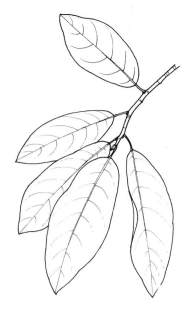

The smooth-margined, simple, oval leaves of the Black Tupelo.

GENUS *Davidia*
(after Abbé Armand David, a French missionary and naturalist)

A genus of a single species of medium-sized trees, native to China, with large, oval, simple leaves, and flowers with enormous bracts borne on the ends of drooping stalks.

not been a success when planted outside its native country. But this is far from true of the Tasmanian Blue Gum (*Eucalyptus globulus*) which, of all eucalypts, is the most widely planted overseas. So long ago was it established in India, New Zealand, and California that many inhabitants of those lands consider it to be a native tree when, actually, it grows naturally only in south Tasmania and on a small peninsula in south Victoria. There it can be up to 54 metres (180 feet) tall with rough, persistent bark at the base of the trunk, shed in strips from the rest of the tree leaving smooth, bluish-grey surfaces. The 150-millimetre (6-inch) long, juvenile leaves are oval, clasping the stem, and covered by a grey, waxy bloom, whereas the adult ones are sometimes 300 millimetres (12 inches) long, curved, and lance shaped. The timber is used for telegraph poles, piles, and railway sleepers. The tree grows remarkably quickly, especially in early life; heights of 16 metres (53 feet) in three years have been recorded in southern India.

A species widely cultivated as an ornamental is the Red-flowering Gum (*Eucalyptus ficifolia*), which has a very restricted natural range along an 80-kilometre (50-mile) long coastal strip in the Albany–Denmark area of south Western Australia. Here, it grows in dense thickets and is rarely more than 7·5 metres (25 feet) tall. But when planted singly in parks and gardens, as it is in many subtropical countries, it forms a small, round-crowned tree covered in scarlet, feathery flowers, the colouring being in the massed filaments of the stamens.

Far left
The quick-growing Tasmanian Blue Gum has been planted in many parts of the world for shade and shelter as well as timber production.

Left
The blossoms of the Red-flowering Gum smother the whole crown of the tree.

The oval, juvenile leaves (*top*), the lance-shaped, mature leaves, and the spinning top-shaped fruit of the Tasmanian Blue Gum.

Left
River Gums are usually found along water courses in the driest area.

Top
The fluffy, round flowers of the Cider Gum are typical of the eucalypts.

Above
The bark of the Ghost Gum is a brilliant white from the bole to the top of the crown.

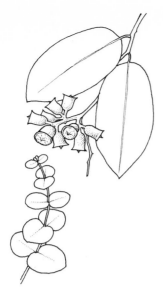

The round, juvenile leaves (*bottom*), the broad, oblong, adult leaves, and the bell-shaped fruits of the Cider Gum.

The red, feathery filaments of the branched flowers and the smooth leaves of the New Zealand Christmas Tree.

The New Zealand Christmas Tree is one of the country's floral delights with its whole crown a solid mass of red flowers in December.

With a very wide range in the arid regions right across north and central Australia is the Coolibah (*Eucalyptus microtheca*), of 'Waltzing Matilda' fame. A small tree about 21 metres (70 feet) tall, with persistent black bark and narrow, evenly grey-green leaves, it is usually found growing beside seasonally inundated streams and backwaters providing shade and shelter for early travellers and prospectors.

A characteristic species of the Northern Territory is the Ghost Gum (*Eucalyptus papuana*), which also occurs around Port Moresby in Papua. It is usually about 18 metres (60 feet) tall and the bark throughout the tree is smooth, shining white, and a remarkable sight in contrast with the greens of the surrounding bush after the rains and the red, lateritic soil in which it often grows.

A hardy species, which has been planted in Europe and other cool temperate regions, is the Cider Gum (*Eucalyptus gunnii*), a native of Tasmania's mountains and growing at altitudes between 600 and 1200 metres (2000 and 4000 feet) where it is seldom more than 24 metres (80 feet) tall, but in Britain a tree of 33.4 metres (110 feet) has been recorded. The bark is persistent at the base of old trees but peels off in strips from the rest of the trunk and branches leaving whitish, smooth areas. The 75-millimetre (3-inch) long, adult leaves are lance shaped and a blue-grey colour all over.

A member of the same family and in a closely related genus is the Pohutukawa (*Metrosideros excelsa*), or New Zealand Christmas Tree. It is one of the floral delights of that country when, at Christmas time, its whole, broad crown is a solid mass of red flowers. Open grown, it stands about 18 metres (60 feet) tall usually with a short trunk and spreading crown with lance-shaped, leathery green leaves, the under surfaces coated with white hairs. The flowers, on terminal heads, in bunches of three each 75 millimetres (3 inches) across, gain their red, feathery appearance from their long stamen filaments. It is a coastal tree from North Island, often forming thickest along the cliff tops, but is planted as an ornamental in most warmer parts of the country.

Family Cornaceae
GENUS *Cornus* dogwoods
(the old Latin name for the Cornelean Cherry, *Cornus mas*)

A genus of about forty species of mostly deciduous, small trees and shrubs, from northern temperate regions, normally with opposite, simple leaves, small flowers sometimes surrounded by large bracts, and fruit in the form of berries.

The only European species which makes a small tree some 7·5 metres (25 feet) tall, and that only occasionally, is the Cornelean Cherry (*Cornus mas*), which is native to southern Europe and western Asia.

The golden flowers of the Cornelian Cherry are early to come out in the spring, long before the leaves.

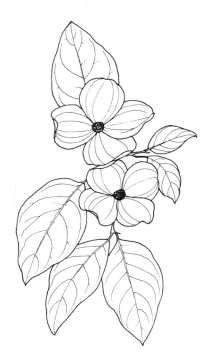

The smooth, oval leaves and the 150-millimetre (6-inch) wide flowers of the Pacific Dogwood.

Above
The Pacific Dogwood is the unofficial national flower of British Columbia.

Below
The white, heath-like flowers of the Strawberry Tree open at the same time as the rough, round, red fruits of the previous year are ripening.

The small, yellow flowers are borne in clusters on the leafless stems in February. It is one of the earliest trees to flower and later produces, among the oval leaves, bright-red, cherry-like fruits which are just edible.

The eastern American species is the Flowering Dogwood (*Cornus florida*), which ranges from southern Maine to southern Ontario, south to Texas and down the east coast to central Florida. On good sites it can be 12 metres (40 feet) tall with a short trunk, clad in bark like an alligator's hide. The oval, rather pointed, bright-green leaves open at the same time or a little later than the four-petalled (actually bracts), 100-millimetre (4-inch), white flowers which are produced in a profusion that makes this one of the most beautiful of spring flowering trees. The red berries which ripen in October are only a little less showy than the flowers. The western species is the Pacific Dogwood (*Cornus nuttallii*), which is native from Vancouver Island south to lower California, reaching its maximum development in the Douglas Fir and Redwood forests, where it is often up to 15 metres (50 feet) tall. The reddish-brown bark is smooth and the oval leaves are not as pointed as the eastern species. The flowers are also larger, up to 150 millimetres (6 inches) across and usually with six rather than four white bracts, tinged with pink. Often the tree flowers twice, the second batch appearing at the same time as the dense clusters of red berries ripen, providing a fine display. This tree is the unofficial national flower of British Columbia.

Bentham's Cornel (*Cornus capitata*), a native of the eastern Himalayas and western China, is a small, bushy tree up to 12 metres (40 feet) tall bearing masses of flowers with pale-yellow bracts which, although much smaller than those of the American species, make a remarkable showing. The fruits are red and fleshy like strawberries.

A Japanese species, also found in China and the Himalayas, (*Cornus controversa*), differs from the others mentioned in having alternative leaves borne at the ends of the twigs and spread out in all directions, and small, white flowers on spreading heads without the large bracts. It is common in Japan as a tree up to 18 metres (60 feet) tall and the timber is used for turnery and carving. The fruits are purplish-black berries.

Family Ericaceae
GENUS *Arbutus* strawberry trees
(the Latin name for the European species)

A genus of twelve species of evergreen trees and shrubs, native to North America, Ireland, and southern Europe, with simple, leathery leaves, pitcher-shaped flowers on terminal stalks, and round, fleshy fruits.

The Strawberry Tree (*Arbutus unedo*) is native to southern Ireland and to the Mediterranean region. It is a wide-crowned tree up to 12 metres (40 feet) tall on a short bole with dark-red bark becoming greyer and scaly with age. The leaves are 100 millimetres (4 inches) long and narrowly oval, with very dark-green upper surfaces and pale green beneath. The white, heath-like, little flowers, twenty-five to thirty on a drooping stalk, open severally in October and November, at the same time as the rough, round, red fruits are ripening from the previous year's flowers. They are edible but unpleasant to taste. The Cyprus Strawberry Tree (*Arbutus andrachne*), native to the eastern Mediterranean, is a similar-sized tree with reddish bark which is shed to reveal pinkish and yellowish areas, especially on the branches. The leaves are broader than the previous species and the smoother, orange-red fruit is smaller. A hybrid between the two species *Arbutus* x *andrachnoides*, with many intermediate characteristics, and particularly handsome, ruby red bark, was first found in Greece.

The largest of the genus is the Madrona (*Arbutus menziesii*), which occurs naturally along the Pacific coast from Vancouver Island to southern California, reaching over 30 metres (100 feet) in height in the lowland fog belt of northern California in company with Redwoods and Douglas Fir but abundant as a small tree even on rocky mountain slopes up to 1200 metres (4000 feet) elevation. The bark, smooth and red in young trees, is sloughed in thin, scaly plates later to reveal smooth, pinkish areas. The attractive stem and branches are matched by the dark-green, lustrous leaves which are the palest of greens below, and the little, white flowers, which are borne on upright stems, are followed by bright orange-red berries, much smaller than those of the other species. The hard, heavy timber is turned and carved into 'novelties' for the tourist trade.

The dark-green, leathery leaves and the round, red fruits of the Strawberry Tree.

The red bark of the Madrona contrasts with the dark-green, lustrous leaves.

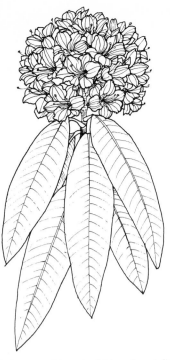

GENUS *Rhododendron*
(from *rhodon*, a rose and *dendron*, a tree)

A genus of over 500 species of flowering shrubs, and a few trees, from north temperate regions, mainly the Himalayas and China, with simple, evergreen or deciduous leaves and funnel- or bell-shaped flowers, usually borne on terminal clusters.

A small tree up to 15 metres (50 feet) tall, widespread in the Himalayas is *Rhododendron arboreum*, with a sturdy trunk and a broad crown of thick, oval, evergreen leaves. Even at 3000 metres (10 000 feet), this tree in April becomes a mass of blood-red flowers borne on thick, round heads 150 millimetres (6 inches) across. Growing on steep hillsides or atop ridges with a background of blue sky and the shimmering white of the eternal snows it makes an unforgettable sight. From this species and many others, hundreds of hybrids and cultivars have been developed, and rhododendrons including their deciduous types, called azaleas, are, after roses, among the most popular of garden plants.

Family Ebenaceae
GENUS *Diospyros*
(from *dios*, godly, and *puros*, wheat grain)

A genus of 200 species of evergreen and deciduous trees, mostly native to the tropics but some from temperate regions of America and Asia, with simple leaves, male flowers in clusters, females single, and the fruit a juicy or leathery berry.

The thick, round head of blood-red flowers and the leathery evergreen leaves of the *Rhododendron arboreum*.

Far left
In April, near Darjeeling in the Himalayas, the Rhododendrons are a mass of pink flowers.

Left
An Ebony tree reaches above the jungle canopy in Mauritius.

Below
The flowers of the Snowbell Tree hang from the branches in little bunches below the leaves.

The Ceylon Ebony (*Diospyros ebenum*), from Sri Lanka and southern India, is the chief source of ebony which is the black heartwood of this species and others of the genus. It is some 18 metres (60 feet) tall and a rather gloomy tree with a dense crown of dark-green, elliptical leaves 75 millimetres (3 inches) long. The jet-black wood is used for piano keys, chessmen, cutlery handles, and much else.

The only New World species of importance is the Persimmon (*Diospyros virginiana*), a native of the eastern states from Connecticut south along the Appalachians and into Texas. It is sometimes over 30 metres (100 feet) tall, but usually much smaller, and has oval, deciduous, 6-inch leaves which are dark green and lustrous. The male and female flowers are on separate trees, the latter producing the 50-millimetre (2-inch) long, plum-like fruits, orange coloured and sweet to taste only after ripening by frost action. The very hard timber was once used for golf club heads.

Family Styracaceae
GENUS *Styrax*
(from the Greek name for these plants)

A genus of over 100 species of small, deciduous trees and shrubs, native to Eurasia and North America, with oval leaves with star-shaped groups of hairs in vein axils on the undersides, white, five-petalled flowers, and egg-shaped fruits.

The Snowbell Tree (*Styrax japonica*) is a native of Japan, Korea, and north-east China, and a handsome flowering tree up to 9 metres (30 feet) tall. The oval leaves, with small, glandular teeth on the margins, are shiny green above and grey-green beneath, and the small, white flowers hang from the branches below the leaves in little bunches on short stalks. The greenish-grey, egg-shaped fruits, about 13 millimetres

Above
The Snowdrop Tree's blossoms hang
evenly spaced along the branches and
very much resemble those of the
garden flower.

Right
The Common Ash is a large tree with a
rather sparse crown of compound
leaves.

The long, compound leaf and the seed
branches ('keys') of the Common Ash.

($\frac{1}{2}$ inch) long, also hang below the branches, splitting in the autumn to
reveal dark-brown nuts. The rather larger Big-leaved Storax (*Styrax
obassia*), native exclusively to Japan, has much wider leaves covered on
the undersides with dense, star-shaped hairs, and the flowers are borne
on stalks at the ends of the branches, not hanging beneath them. Of the
two species, the latter is the more popular among Japanese gardeners.
Both of them grow in the cool, moist woods of central and southern
Japan.

A larger but very similar and closely related tree of another genus
is the American Snowdrop Tree (*Halesia monticola*), native to, and found
at altitudes of around 900 metres (3000 feet) on, the mountains of
North Carolina, eastern Tennessee, and western Georgia. Much larger
than the *Styrax* species, sometimes up to 24 metres (80 feet) tall, it has
narrower, more pointed leaves, but still the white, drooping flowers
hanging from the branches, although the fruit is quite different and is
50 millimetres (2 inches) long, 13 millimetres ($\frac{1}{2}$ inch) wide, brown and
dry with four wings.

Family Oleaceae
GENUS *Fraxinus* ash trees
(the old Latin name for ash trees)

A genus of over sixty species of large, deciduous trees, nearly all from
northern temperate regions, with opposite, compound leaves, petalless
flowers pollinated by the wind, and winged fruits.

The Common Ash (*Fraxinus excelsior*) is one of Europe's largest
deciduous trees and distributed throughout the continent as well as in
Asia Minor. Trees up to 30 metres (100 feet) tall are common, and heights
of 42 metres (140 feet) are recorded. The pale-grey, smooth bark in
young trees gives way to deeply fissured bark in later life. The black
winter buds are very characteristic, and are among the last to open in
the spring to produce the 300-millimetre (12-inch) compound leaves
each with nine to thirteen leaflets which are among the first to fall in the
autumn. The purple flowers open before the leaves and give way to
bunches of 'keys' which hang on the tree long after the leaves have gone.
Although usually seen as a hedgerow tree, the Ash is also cultivated for
its excellent, tough, white timber which is made into hockey sticks and
other sports goods as well as tool handles and, according to prevailing
fashion, furniture. The Weeping Ash, cultivar 'Pendula', common
in parks and gardens, has branches which arch out and grow straight

Right
The yellow, feathery flowers of the
Flowering Ash appear in June after the
leaves have opened.

Below
Olive groves have been cultivated in
Europe for at least 5000 years.

down to the ground, usually grafted on to the bole of a type tree. The Flowering Ash (*Fraxinus ornus*), from southern Europe and western Asia, is a smaller, denser-crowned tree with grey buds. The leaves are shorter, with five to nine leaflets, but it is the beautiful, yellowy white, feathery flowers, appearing after the leaves, which give this tree its undoubted attraction and its popularity as an ornamental.

The American White Ash (*Fraxinus americana*) ranges from Nova Scotia west to Minnesota and southwards to Texas and Florida, and is the largest and finest of the ashes in that country, reaching 36 metres (120 feet) tall in fertile parts of the Ohio valley. The tree has a more compact, oval crown than the common species, and the 38-millimetre (15-inch) long leaves have seven to nine stalked leaflets which are whitish on the undersides. The Red Ash (*Fraxinus pennsylvanica*), with a distribution extending further north-east into Alberta and Montana, is a smaller tree with more pointed, narrower leaflets whereas the Oregon Ash (*Fraxinus oregona*) has rounder leaflets, especially the terminal one, which are yellow-green above and paler and downy beneath. The timber of the American ashes is used for the same purposes as that of the European species.

The Manchurian Ash (*Fraxinus mandshurica*), native to Japan, Manchuria, and north-eastern China, is closely related to the European Common Ash but has more slender leaflets which are tapered to the base. And the Chinese Flowering Ash (*Fraxinus mariesii*) is very similar to the European flowering species except that its fruits turn an attractive purple in July providing a second display after the yellow flowers.

GENUS *Olea* olives
(the Latin name for the olive)

A genus of some twenty species of evergreen trees from Europe, Asia, and Australasia, with simple leaves, flowers on stalks rising from the leaf axils, and fruit in the form of a pulpy berry with a single stone.

The Common Olive (*Olea europaea*), which is cultivated throughout the Mediterranean region and in many other countries, probably came originally from Asia Minor. There is archaeological evidence that Olive orchards existed in Crete in 3500 BC. It is a somewhat straggling tree, up to 12 metres (40 feet) tall, with grey-green, leathery, lance-shaped leaves and small, green, fragrant flowers. The fruits, the olives, take about a year to ripen when they turn black and contain up to 30 per cent of oil. The green table olives must be picked before they are ripe and be subject to a process lasting six months to remove the substances which make them so bitter as to be inedible. Olive trees are very long lived and specimens of over 1000 years old are known to exist. There are frequent references to them in the Bible.

Family Apocynaceae
GENUS *Plumeria*
(after Charles Plumier, a French botanist)

A genus of ten species of evergreen trees, from tropical America, with thick, fleshy branches, large elliptical leaves and large fragrant flowers. The fruits are long pods.

The Frangipani (*Plumeria acuminata*) is a native of Mexico but is planted throughout the tropics. A spreading tree up to 9 metres (30 feet) tall, it has thick branches and twigs from which a latex flows copiously if wounded, and shiny, heavily veined leaves about 380 millimetres (15 inches) long. The waxy, white flowers, each about 75 millimetres (3 inches) across, are borne on heads of as many as six flowers each, and have a fragrance, almost sickly in its sweetness, which is wafted great distances from the tree. The flowers are made into wreaths and garlands, and few ceremonies take place in the tropics unaccompanied by the heavy scent of this tree.

Family Scrophulariaceae
GENUS *Paulownia*
(after Princess Anna Paulowna, daughter of Csar Paul I)

A genus of ten species of deciduous trees, native to eastern Asia, with large, long-stalked, simple leaves, and tubular flowers on a terminal head.

The Foxglove Tree (*Paulownia tomentosa*), a native of China, is a

The thick twigs, leathery leaves, and large, perfumed flowers of the Frangipani.

The waxy flowers of the Frangipani have a fragrance almost sickly in its sweetness.

somewhat sparsely branched tree, up to 15 metres (50 feet) tall, with large, heart-shaped leaves 250 millimetres (10 inches) long, slightly hairy above and densely so beneath. The purple- to violet-coloured flowers are shaped like large foxgloves and are borne on erect stems 300 millimetres (12 inches) long, making it one of the most striking of flowering trees. The fruits are pale green and egg shaped with a sharp point at the top. Unfortunately not very hardy, it is rarely seen flowering in Britain except in the extreme south; and in eastern America, where it is a very popular ornamental, it does not do well north of New York.

Family Bignoniaceae
GENUS *Catalpa*
(from the North American Indian name for the tree)

A genus of ten species of medium-sized, deciduous trees, native to North America, the West Indies, and eastern Asia, with large, opposite, simple leaves, bell-shaped flowers on terminal stalks, and fruits in the form of long, slender, cylindrical pods.

The largest of the genus is the Western Catalpa (*Catalpa speciosa*) which has a rather restricted range centred round the confluence of the Ohio and Mississippi rivers, and is a tree typical of the bottom lands of the Ohio basin in southern Illinois and Indiana. Open grown, the tree reaches a height of some 18 metres (60 feet) with a broad, spreading crown of pointed, heart-shaped leaves up to 300 millimetres (12 inches) long. The white, brown-spotted, bell-shaped flowers with frilly rims are

Erect at first, the flower stems of the Foxglove Tree soon hang down from the weight of the pale purple blossoms.

The lobed, young leaf and the erect bunch of purplish flowers of the Foxglove Tree.

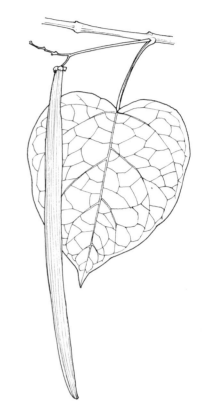

The pods of the Indian Bean Tree are up to 0·6 metre (2 feet) long and hang on the tree like black bootlaces far into the winter.

The prominent veined leaf and slender, cylindrical seed pod of the Indian Bean Tree.

borne in dense clusters on erect stems at the ends of the twigs and make a remarkable show in June and July. The fruit pods, which are nearly 0·6 metre (2 feet) long and very slender, eventually turn black and hang on the tree all winter, bursting in the spring to produce quantities of small, flat, winged seeds. With a more southerly range, from Florida westwards to Mississippi, the Indian Bean Tree (*Catalpa bignonioides*), is a lesser tree with smaller, blunter leaves but with many more flowers on each spike, spotted with yellow and purple. The fruit pods are slimmer even than those of the western species and look like boot laces hanging in bunches on the bare winter branches.

The Yellow Catalpa (*Catalpa ovata*), from northern China, is a tree about 15 metres (50 feet) tall with tripointed, dark-green leaves and yellow flowers; and Farges Catalpa (*Catalpa fargesii*), from western China, has very pointed, heart-shaped leaves and pink flowers.

GENUS *Jacaranda*
(a Latinized form of the Brazilian name for these trees)

A genus of some forty species of medium-sized, mostly deciduous trees and shrubs, native to Brazil, with compound, feathery leaves, narrow, bell-shaped flowers, developing into wavy-edged, disc-like pods containing two-winged seeds.

Jacaranda acutifolia is the best known of the genus and is a deciduous tree up to 18 metres (60 feet) tall, with doubly compound, feathery leaves and bearing large clusters of blue- to violet-coloured flowers. It is one of the most spectacular of flowering trees and, when planted in street avenues, as it is in many subtropical countries, it provides a display which is one of the annual highlights.

Family Rubiaceae
GENUS *Coffea*
(from the Arabic *kahwa*, coffee)

A genus of forty species of small, tropical, evergreen trees, from Africa and Asia, with glossy, elliptical leaves, white, fragrant flowers and fruit in the form of berries.

The most important species is the Arabian Coffee (*Coffea arabica*), a native of Ethiopa, and a tree up to 15 metres (50 feet) tall with long, pointed, glossy green leaves, and dense clusters of jasmine-scented, white flowers borne in the leaf axils. These produce the berries, which are green at first becoming purple, each containing two seeds, the kernels of which are the coffee 'beans'. They must be roasted before they have the coffee flavour. In plantations, the trees are pruned to keep them

The compound, feathery leaf and the cluster of violet-coloured flowers of the Jacaranda.

215

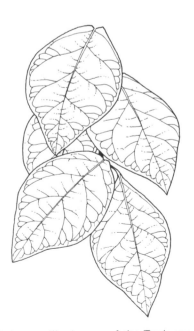

Above
The small flowers of the Teak are borne in large bunches at the ends of the branches.

Above right
The *Jacaranda* is one of the most spectacular of trees for urban planting in subtropical countries.

Right
Teak trees usually grow scattered singly over wide areas of forest, and elephants are often the only means of transporting them.

The tobacco-like leaves of the Teak are 0·6 metre (2 feet) long and 380 millimetres (15 inches) wide.

low and accessible; and one tree will only produce about a kilogram (2 pounds) of beans (after roasting) in a year, so that the plantations must be very extensive. Brazil and Colombia are the most important coffee-producing countries even though no coffee trees are native to the New World.

Family Verbenaceae
GENUS *Tectona* teak
(from *tekton*, a carpenter)

A genus of three species of large, deciduous trees, native to the Indo-Malaysia region, with very large, simple leaves, small flowers in large, spreading terminal bunches, and small fruits with a papery covering.

The Teak (*Tectona grandis*), one of the world's best-known timber trees, is a native of Burma, Thailand, Java, and the Philippines. It is a large tree up to 30 metres (100 feet) tall, with a fluted base to the trunk and enormous, tobacco-like leaves 0·6 metre (2 feet) long and 380 millimetres (15 inches) wide. In the monsoon forests, it seldom grows in pure stands but is usually scattered over wide areas mixed with other species, and elephants are often the only means of dragging the individual logs to a central point. Teak timber is extremely durable and hard, requiring no painting or preservatives, and has long been used for ship-building, piles, road surfacing, garden seats, and many other outdoor uses where unmaintained permanence is desired.

Family Palmae palms

A family of 2600 species of tropical, subtropical, and warm temperate plants of which some have massive, solid stems, without secondary thickening or branches, topped by a crown of spirally arranged, persistent, stiff leaves.

GENUS *Phoenix*

A genus of seventeen species of feather-leaved palms, the leaflets with pointed tips.

By far the best known and most useful of this genus is the Date Palm (*Phoenix dactylifera*), a tree found growing from west Africa to India. Its stout, rough trunk, covered with persistent leaf bases, holds the large crown of stiff, spreading, 6-metre (20-feet) long, grey-green leaves 30 metres (100 feet) or so above the ground. The female tree bears up to 10 000 flowers on each hanging cluster; from these, fleshy fruits are formed. A single tree may bear up to 45 kilograms (100 pounds) of fruit yearly for over a century. No wild tree has ever been found, but the Date Palm is known to have been in the Middle East since 5000 BC. The so-called Wild Date Palm (*Phoenix sylvestris*) of India is very like *P. dactilifera* and is generally supposed to have been its ancestor. Other members of the genus are tapped for their sweet sap which is made into sugar and wine.

GENUS *Cocos*

A genus of one species of tall, smooth-stemmed palms with crowns of between twenty-five to thirty-six leaves, each with seventy to 100 pairs of leaflets.

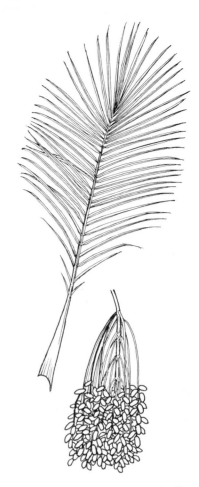

The grey-green, sharp-pointed leaflets on the huge, 6-metre (20-feet) long leaf of the Date Palm and bunched fruit.

The dark-green, softish leaflets of the Coconut and the big nut in its fibrous husk.

A single Date Palm may produce up to 45 kilograms (100 pounds) of fruit yearly for over a century.

217

Palm

The Coconut Palm (*Cocos nucifera*), one of the most useful trees in the world, is found throughout the tropics, usually along the seashore and never very far inland. Like the Date Palm, its wild origin is unknown, but all evidence suggests that it came from the ancient Pacific or even from the west coast of South America, its huge 'nuts' carried by ocean currents from island to island, until man realized its value and planted it throughout the tropical world. The coconut, inside a fibrous husk, takes six months to reach its full size and another four to ripen. For processing, the ripe nuts are split and the halves are exposed to the sun. When dry, the 'meat' is the copra from which oil is extracted for cooking oil, soap, and margarine; the grated copra is used by confectioners; the fibrous husks produce coir from which ropes, matting and bags are made; and the shells are made into bowls, spoons, toys, and the finest medicinal charcoal. The trunks of old trees are used in house building. The annual harvest of copra is three million tonnes.

GENUS *Elaeis*

A cocoid genus differing from *Cocos* in having the trunk covered with the remnant stumps of the fallen leaves which themselves have 100 to 160 leaflets.

The Oil Palm (*Elaeis guineensis*) is found in swamps and low-lying land throughout tropical Africa, including Madagascar, and grows to between 24 to 30 metres (80 and 100 feet) tall. A single tree will bear anything up to 4000 small, cherry-like fruits each year, weighing something like 27 kilograms (60 pounds). The pulpy pericarp and the stone which it surrounds both contain oil which is extracted by pressing. The oil has a great similarity to olive oil and has more uses than coconut oil. And, as the fruits ripen in half the time of the coconut oil, palm plantations are being established in many countries beyond Africa.

GENUS *Washingtonia*

A genus of stout palms with trunks covered in persistent, dead leaves, and with fan-shaped leaves.

The Californian Fan Palm (*Washington filifera*) is native to isolated, dry areas in California, Arizona, and Mexico, where it grows to some 24 metres (80 feet) tall with a massive trunk made more so in its upper half by a skirt of dead, drooping leaves, supporting a crown of grey-

Far left
Coconut Palms usually grow along the seashore and are never found far inland.

Below
A single Oil Palm bears anything up to 4000 small, cherry-like fruits each year.

Below left
The tall, slender Sealing Wax Palms have scarlet leaf sheaths at the tops of their stems.

green, fan-shaped leaves. This skirt of dried leaves, which completely covers the trunk of young trees is an insulating device in these palms which have to contend with a cold spell of weather each year. When planted in avenues they make an imposing sight.

California Fan Palms make attractive street trees with their dense heads of fan-like leaves.

GENUS *Trachycarpus*

A genus of temperate climate palms with rough, fibrous stems covered with the projecting, woody bases of old leaf stems. The stalks of the fan-shaped leaves are armed with small, sharp spines.

The Windmill Palm (*Trachycarpus fortunei*), a native of southern China, grows to 9 metres (30 feet) tall, and is one of the hardiest palms. It is planted in some gardens in Europe, and even in southern England. The nearly round, yet fan-like leaves about 0·9 metre (3 feet) in diameter, radiate from the top of the stem, from an orb-shaped crown.

Index

221

Acknowledgments

Biofotos: 13T, 15T, 16–17, 18T, 19, 22T + B, 27L + R, 29L + R, 30, 35, 36BL, 41, 45, 52R, 54T + B, 60, 62, 65R, 72, 73, 74, 75L, 76–77, 81, 83, 85T + B, 92B, 92–93, 93T + B, 96, 97T, 99, 103, 105, 106, 114, 115B, 118, 120, 121, 122, 128, 130, 142, 147, 162, 162–163, 165, 174, 178, 179R, 184, 185BR, 188, 189, 193T, 195, 206T, 209T, 212B, 217, 219; Bruce Coleman Ltd: 173; M Boulton 86; J Markham 22BR; N Myers 48; Lee Rue 179L; W F Davidson: 21, 37B, 94, 149T, 154R, 156; S Leathart: 23T + B, 34, 38, 44T, 51, 59, 64, 69, 80, 82, 116–117, 125, 159, 160T + B, 180; Natural History Photographic Agency: Front and back jacket, jacket flaps, endpapers, 10, 32, 37T, 42, 43, 44B, 46, 50, 56, 57T + B, 65L, 67, 70L, 78, 79, 92T, 97B, 98R, 100, 107, 109, 112, 113, 115T, 123L + R, 124, 127, 132, 134, 139T, 140B, 141, 143, 145L + R, 148, 157R, 161, 170L, 171, 177, 180–181, 194, 196, 197R, 200, 203T, 205, 211, 212T, 213, 215, 219TL; H R Allen 52L, 140T; D Baglin 198, 203B; A Bannister 28; K A + G Beckett 33, 90R, 210; S Dalton 26L + R, 31, 36TL, 49, 100–101, 186; M Davies 187; D Dickens 63, 192, 208; J B Free 191; B Hawkes 24L, 108R; Horticultural Photographic Collection 193B; A Huxley 20, 146, 206B, 209B; G E Hyde 61, 98L, 104L, 110, 129, 133, 149B, 153T, 155, 158, 185T; P Johnson 218; A Mitchell 38–39, 40L, 47, 55, 75R, 84, 87, 88, 89L + R 102, 104R, 108L, 182; M K Morcombe 15B, 199; F Naylor 201, 204; L H Newman 40R; M Nimmo 13B; I Polunin 90L, 175, 190, 216L, 219R; E H Rao 16, 219BL; M Savonius 111, 153B, 172; H Smith 36TR, 53, 66, 68, 70R, 71, 119, 131, 135, 136, 138, 139B, 150, 151, 154L, 157L, 164L + R, 166, 167, 168, 169, 170R, 176, 183, 197L, 207, 214, 220; P Wayne 24R; Royal Forestry Society Slide Library: 11, 18B; Tony Stone Associates: endpapers, 12, 14, 95, 202.